Other Books by Charles P. Curtis:

HUNTING IN AFRICA, EAST AND WEST
(with Richard C. Curtis)

INTRODUCTION TO PARETO
(with George C. Homans)

THE PRACTICAL COGITATOR
(with Ferris Greenslet)

LIONS UNDER THE THRONE

IT'S YOUR LAW

THE MODERN PRUDENT INVESTOR

THE OPPENHEIMER CASE: THE TRIAL OF A
SECURITY SYSTEM

A COMMONPLACE BOOK

LAW
AS LARGE
AS LIFE

A Natural Law for Today

And the Supreme Court As Its Prophet

by CHARLES P. CURTIS

SIMON AND SCHUSTER
NEW YORK · 1959

THE GASPAR G. BACON LECTURESHIP

This volume comprises the three lectures delivered by Charles P. Curtis at Boston University in the Gaspar G. Bacon Lecture series in October 1958.

The lectureship was endowed in 1927 by Mrs. Robert Bacon of New York in honor of her son, Gaspar G. Bacon. A Boston lawyer, Mr. Bacon was active in both public affairs and academic life. He served several terms in the legislature and a term as Lieutenant Governor of the Commonwealth of Massachusetts. He was a Lieutenant Colonel in Military Government in the European theater during World War II. Just prior to the war he had been professor and Chairman of the Department of Government at Boston University. The lectureship is a memorial to his accomplishments in public life and academic affairs and his interest in the Constitution of the United States.

The purpose of the lectureship is to stimulate a study of the Constitution of the United States, its history, doctrines, and implications. Each year a recognized statesman, jurist, or scholar is invited to deliver the lectures in this series.

The author wishes to express his gratitude to the following individuals and publishers for permission to include material in this book from the following sources:

Selections reprinted from *The Astonished Muse,* by Reuel Denney, by permission of The University of Chicago Press, © 1957 by The University of Chicago.

The Belknap Press of Harvard University Press for selections from *The Unpublished Opinions of Mr. Justice Brandeis,* by A. M. Bickel, © 1957 by The President and Fellows of Harvard College.

Reinhold Niebuhr and *The Christian Century* for "Proposal to Billy Graham," by Reinhold Niebuhr; and The Fund for the Republic for a Mike Wallace interview with Reinhold Niebuhr.

Oxford University Press for selections from *Historical Inevitability*, by Isaiah Belin, 1954.

Philosophical Library for selections from *Words and Their Uses*, by Stephen Ullman, © 1951 by Philosophical Library; and for selections from *Science and Philosophy*, by Alfred North Whitehead, © 1948 by Philosophical Library.

Secker and Warburg for selections from "Philosophy at Absolute Zero," by Professor A. J. Ayer, from *Encounter*, October 1955.

Charles Scribner's Sons for selections from *Axel's Castle*, by Edmund Wilson, © 1931 by Charles Scribner's Sons; renewal © 1959 by Edmund Wilson.

Willis Kingsley Wing for selections from *Battle for the Mind*, by William Sargant, © 1957 by William Sargant, reprinted by permission of Willis Kingsley Wing.

C. Vann Woodward for selections from "Equality," from *The American Scholar*.

To Learned Hand

As the appearance of the bow that is in the cloud in the day of rain, so was the appearance of the brightness round about. This was the appearance of the likeness of the glory of the Lord. And when I saw it, I fell upon my face, and I heard a voice of one that spake.

And he said unto me, Son of man, stand upon thy feet, and I will speak unto thee.

EZEKIEL, 1:28; 2:1

LAW

AS LARGE

AS LIFE

I

IN JUSTICE HOLMES'S house at Beverly Farms, on the parlor wall, at the left, as I recall it, of the fireplace, there hung a framed photograph of an open field. There was nothing conspicuous in it except a wooden sign on a post. This sign read: THIS IS THE EQUATOR. Many years later its significance occurred to me. Aside from the sign's own assertion, there was no reason at all to think that this *was* the equator. The photograph might just as well have been taken in the field near the house.

So I ask you, do not believe anything I say. Examine it. Socrates told his judges that the unexamined life was not worth living. Nor is an unexamined thought worth thinking. Take nothing I say on faith, no more than Holmes believed what the sign said.

I am taking my departure from a bearing on one of the great headlands in the Holmes lectures Learned Hand gave in 1958. (Harvard University Press, 1958.) This headland is the position Hand takes on the doctrine of judicial supremacy. Hand says that if we set aside any kind of natural law, both that of St. Thomas Aquinas and that of our Thomas Jefferson, the Supreme Court has no warrant of authority to hold an act of Congress or any State statute unconstitutional. And yet it was not "a lawless act to import into the Constitution such a grant of power" to the Court to decide whose decision should be final, the President's, or Congress', or a State's. For it was "necessary to prevent the failure of the undertaking for the Supreme Court to assume an authority to keep the States, Congress, and the President within their prescribed powers." "Otherwise," Hand goes on, "the government could not proceed as planned; and indeed would almost certainly have foundered." The doctrine of judicial supremacy is warranted, but its only warrant is necessity.

But the Supreme Court assumed a further authority, by what Hand calls a *coup de main*, to tell the other departments of our government *how* as well as *what* each might do. There was no warrant of necessity for this. It was a *coup de main* when the Court assumed the role of a third legislative chamber and undertook to annul any legislation because the Court disapproved of it on its merits. An unwarranted *coup de main*. "Nevertheless," Hand concedes, "it is desirable that they should exercise such an authority on extreme occasions."

Extreme occasions have a way of taking care of themselves. They take charge. I am interested in something more amenable.

Hand said, "I cannot frame any definition that will explain when the Court will assume the role of a third legislative chamber and when it will limit its authority to keeping Congress and the States within their accredited authority." He put aside, remember, any kind of Natural Law, any "code of paramount law that not only measured the scope of legislative authority but regulated how it should be exercised."

Is there no definition, no principle, no doctrine which will explain and thereby determine when the Court is stepping beyond the necessity which is its only justification, beyond *what* the Congress and the States and the President are doing to trespass on *how* they are doing it? Let us satisfy ourselves. Is there any?

In the old days, before the New Deal gave us a New Court, I don't think it had occurred to many of the Justices that there was any problem. They bridled when Stone, Brandeis, and Cardozo—a formidable trio—told them, back in 1936, in the A.A.A. case (297 U.S. 1), "The only check upon our own exercise of power is our own sense of self-restraint. For the removal of unwise laws from the statute books appeal lies not to the courts but to the ballot and to the processes of democratic government." The best reply they could make is more revealing than intelligible. After all, everything we say is one or the other. What they said was this (300 U.S. at 402) :

"The suggestion that the only check upon the exercise of the judicial power, when properly invoked, to declare a constitutional right superior to an unconstitutional statute is the judge's own self-restraint, is both ill considered and mischievous. Self-restraint belongs in the domain of will and not of judgment. The check upon the judge is that imposed by his oath of office, by the Constitution, and by his own conscientious and informed convictions; and since he has the duty to make up his own mind and adjudge accordingly, it is hard to see how there could be any other restraint."

I remember how illuminating Justice Harlan Stone's remark seemed. It was some years later that I began to understand that Stone had only stated the problem, whose existence the older Justices had been denying. For the need of self-restraint does, indeed, recognize that the Court has a power which needs to be restrained.

Justice Felix Frankfurter's approach to the problem is more promising. He adds humility. "Our duty to abstain from confounding policy with constitutionality demands perceptive humility as well as self-restraint in not declaring unconstitutional what in a judge's private judgment is unwise and even dangerous." (Dennis v. U.S., 341 U.S. at 552; see also 335 U.S. at 556.) Thoreau was right: "Humility like darkness reveals the heavenly lights." But as a duty it is only a precept to take an attitude. It's not a definition.

Frankfurter, to my mind, comes nearer the mark when he tells us that the Court's role is that of a critic. This is another promising line of thought, but I wonder how far it takes us. How shall a man pass judgment on what another has done without covertly wondering how

he would have done it himself? A judge has the same difficulty dis-
engaging himself from the legislature as a critic has to keep aloof from
the author. As soon as a critic is satisfied that he has got the right
principles of criticism, he can't help seeing how they work. What
Coleridge said of the critic strikes me as equally true of a judge: "The
ultimate end of criticism is much more to establish the principles of
writing than to furnish rules how to pass judgment on what has been
written by others; if indeed it were possible that the two could be separated." (S. T. Coleridge, *Biographia Literaria*, XVIII.)

Hand, I may say, has no doubt. "I do not see how a court can invalidate [statutes] without putting itself in the same position and declaring whether the legislature's substitute is what the court would
have coined to meet the occasion. True, courts might, and indeed they
always do, disclaim authority to intervene unless they are sure beyond
doubt that the compromise imposed is wrong; but that does not dis-
guise the fact that their choice is an authentic exercise of the same
process that produced the statute itself."

Finally, so far as I know, there is the canon of that friend of humanity, the just and yet reasonable man. As Holmes put it, a statute
is not to be held unconstitutional "unless it can be said that a rational
and fair man necessarily would admit that the statute proposed would
infringe fundamental principles as they have been understood by the
traditions of our people and our law." (In his dissent in the *Lochner*
case, 198 U.S. at 74.)

So, when a constitutional question is raised, a judge would do well
to emulate "a fair and rational man," just as a trial judge, sitting without a jury, may try to make his judgment correspond with what he
thinks a jury would do. (Judge Charles E. Wyzanski, Jr., in *A Trial
Judge's Freedom*.) The analogy is not so farfetched as you may be
thinking. Constitutional questions, Brandeis tells us, "resemble fundamentally" questions of negligence, which are ordinarily left to the

verdict of the jury. "In every such case, the decision, in the first instance, is dependent upon the determination of what in legal parlance
is called a fact, as distinguished from the declaration of a rule of
law." (Brandeis, dissenting in *Burnet* v. *Coronado Oil & Gas Co.*, 285
U.S. 393, 1932.)

II

I THINK old Truepenny, that familiar ghost, the fair and rational man, has led us back to the stone which the builder, at least *arguendo*, refused. Let us see if it may not be the headstone in the corner, and if it fits, let us also make sure that we are putting it in the right building.

I am proposing a Natural Law for Today, not a revival of the natural law that Hand rejected, neither that of the Church and St. Thomas Aquinas nor that of the Enlightenment and Thomas Jefferson. I want to propose a version of natural law that is both modern and mundane.

Familiarity with the law sometimes breeds misunderstanding as well as contempt. We are all more or less familiar with the law, in one way or another, and yet we don't all recognize the fact that the law is made up of two very different components. One is positive law. The other is natural law. These are trade names, and outside the trade they are of no help to understanding them or their relation to each other.

To begin with, although there are occasions when these two very different kinds of law diverge and frustrate each other, fortunately for society this is only the dramatic and exceptional case. Their usual and domestic function is to complement and complete each other, like a team of oxen. They are companions, they are brothers, in law. They are the right and left hands of Justice. To speak technically, they are not contraries, they are *sub*contraries.

8

The best way to isolate the positive element in law is to take the point of view of a deliberate wrongdoer who wants to break the law as safely and as cheaply as he can. For the positive law is satisfied with a penalty. It offers an open choice between the prescribed penalty and obedience. It puts a price tag on disobedience.

This is the approach Justice Holmes advised law students to take when studying for their bar examinations. He emphasized the difference between law and morals, and then he went on to say that he did so to the single end of learning and understanding the law. "It is for that that I ask you for the moment to imagine yourselves indifferent to other and greater things. If you want to know the law and nothing else, you must look at it as a bad man who cares only for the material consequences which such knowledge enables him to predict, not as a good one who finds his reasons for conduct, whether inside the law or outside of it, in the vaguer sanctions of conscience."

A purely positive law is, no doubt, the best law for students to begin on. So too it is for lawyers. For there's no need to appeal to justice until the positive law fails them. When you hear a lawyer appealing to the justice of his cause, it's a good guess that the law—that is, the positive law—is against him. The positive law is likewise the law for judges, so far, that is, as it will take them. For they are bound to follow it, whether they like it or not, so far as it goes. But when it fails him, a judge may, because he must, look beyond.

But the law is not made only for students, nor only for lawyers, nor even only for judges. It is our law for us too, and we cannot regard it as just another objective fact in our lives and our careers. Justice is something more than the price of disobedience. There's an *ought* as well as an *is* in the law, and this is where natural law plays its part.

Natural law is harder to describe than its positive counterpart. For natural law has too many facets, too many aspects, to succumb to any single definition, even if a definition ever amounted to an adequate description. Here are a few. From a juristic point of view, we may take it that natural law is made up of those fundamental principles of liberty and justice which Justice Benjamin Cardozo said were "deeply rooted in reason and in the compelling traditions of the legal profession . . . implicit in the concept of ordered liberty." Professor Lon Fuller goes deeper and calls it "the fundamental rules that make law itself possible." Judge Charles E. Wyzanski, Jr., thinks of it as "a set of basic premises," "a core of values," such as are "characteristic of our particular civilization." Professor Benjamin F. Wright uses the word *consensus*. Walter Lippmann is convinced that there is "a body of positive principles and precepts which a good citizen cannot deny or ignore" and calls it "The Public Philosophy." But definitions are but road signs. They tell you which way to go, and at the same time how far distant you are from the City of Understanding. All we need to know at the beginning is what the author is going to talk about. By the time we get through no definition ought to be necessary.

The two I like best, one plain and the other fancy, are these:

Take the plain one first. It is in John Dewey's little book, *The Living Thoughts of Thomas Jefferson* (David McKay, 1940).

"Jefferson used the language of the time in his assertion of 'natural rights' upon which governments are based and which they must observe if they are to have legitimate authority. What is not now so plain is that the word *moral* can be substituted for the word *natural* whenever Jefferson used the latter in connection with law and rights, not only without changing his meaning but making it clearer to a modern reader. Not only does he say: 'I am convinced man has no natural right in opposition to his social duties,' and that 'man was destined for society,' but also that 'questions of natural right are triable by their conformity with the moral sense and reason of man.' "

The other, which is on the fancy side, comes from another great philosopher, Alfred North Whitehead.

"My own belief is that at present the most fruitful, because the most neglected, starting point is that section of value-theory which we term aesthetics. Our enjoyment of the values of human art, or of natural beauty, our horror at the obvious vulgarities and defacements which force themselves upon us—all these modes of experience are sufficiently abstracted to be relatively obvious. And yet evidently they disclose the very meaning of things.

"Habits of thought and sociological habits survive because in some broad sense they promote aesthetic enjoyment. There is an ultimate satisfaction to be derived from them. Thus when the pragmatist asks whether 'it works,' he is asking whether it issues in aesthetic satisfaction. The judge of the Supreme Court is giving his decision on the basis of the aesthetic satisfaction of the harmonization of the American Constitution with the activities of modern America." (*Science and Philosophy*, The Wisdom Library, 1948; p. 138.)

But how futile definitions are! Here again, as so often, the best they can do is to elaborate the notions of those who are already acquainted with what they are defining. Definitions, by and large, are of no help unless you don't need them. Nor are explanations any better to begin with, though they may flatter our understanding if they are philosophic enough. Later, after we have seen and touched the thing itself, they may be of great help. So, instead of putting in here those few that have helped me and suggesting you skip them and come back to them, I have put them into an appendix. There you will find how Whitehead brings symbolism as well as aesthetics to bear, how our natural law may be his "immanent law" and our positive law his "imposed law," why language and grammar may have something to tell us, and why a dominant natural law of the kind we are talking about may be, if Dorothy Lee is right, the soil in which individualism best thrives. Meanwhile, I want to get on with my theme. So I offer you three or four outward signs, what bird-watchers call field marks, by which you will be able to recognize the presence of this natural-law component in a law, and even guess how great it is.

The first is a generality of expression. Natural law is so difficult to put into words that it is only a small exaggeration to call it "the unwritten law." So we take to large terms with little meaning of their own—or, if you prefer, so many meanings that room must be made for them, like Los Angeles, which they call a lot of suburbs looking for a city. Such words as *fair*, or *just*, or *reasonable*, or *due*, or *equal* are sure signs of a natural component; and so too are the great comprehensive commands, like Thou Shalt Not Kill, from which numberless exceptions have to be peeled off before you hang a man for murder. Words like these give us only a direction, not directions. They are compass bearing without pilotage. They are words that await the occasion which will give the meaning, for natural law, come down to it, deals only in particulars and provides only for concrete perplexities.

Another way for a layman to detect the presence of natural law is to ask himself whether he can't perhaps tell his lawyer as much about the law in question as his lawyer can tell him.

In a similar way, lawyers may ask themselves whether it is a matter for the judge to decide or a jury. For, as someone has said, judges find questions of natural law too difficult. Anyhow, they are not the kind a lawyer is specially trained to answer.

I know of one more field mark—the best, I think. It concerns the method of enforcement. If punishment or a penalty for the breach of a law is either ineffective or unnecessary, if force is either futile or worse, then you may be sure that you are dealing with a large component of natural law, which is less amenable to punishment than positive law.

III

THERE WAS ONCE a farm boy in western New York who got a chance to read law in the judge's office at the county seat. His father's farm was some ten miles away, and his father drove the boy in one September day and left him to take up the reading. Three weeks went by before his father drove the team in town again and took him home for Sunday dinner. When the apple pie was finished and the family was still gathered around the table, the farmer asked the boy, "Well, son, how do you like the law?" There was a brief ruminative silence; then the boy said, "Pa, I don't like it. I'm sorry I learned it."

It's an absurd story, if you are thinking of bar examinations. A lifetime is too short nowadays to learn the law. So we have tax lawyers, patent and copyright lawyers, trial lawyers, corporation lawyers, and probate lawyers. What the boy said is funny enough, but don't you detect in yourself a troubling feeling that you too know more law than you know you know?

We all have this feeling, and if we were as candid as the farmer's son was naïve, we would admit it. Thomas Jefferson said, "State a moral case to a ploughman and a professor. The former will decide it as well, and often better than the latter, because he has not been led astray by artificial rules." Perhaps I'd better give the whole passage. Jefferson was writing to his nephew, Peter Carr, from Paris on August 10, 1787, while the Constitutional Convention was in session in Philadelphia:

"I think it is lost time to attend lectures on moral philosophy. He who made us would have been a pitiful bungler if He had made the rules of our moral conduct a matter of science. For one man of science, there are thousands who are not. What would have become of them? Man was destined for society. His morality, therefore, was to be formed to this object. He was endowed with a sense of right and wrong, merely relative to this. This sense is as much a part of his nature as the sense of hearing, seeing, feeling; it is the true foundation of morality, and not the *to kalon*, truth, etc., as fanciful writers have imagined. The moral sense, or conscience, is as much a part of man as his leg or arm. It is given to all human beings in a stronger or weaker degree, as force of members is given them in a greater or less degree. It may be strengthened by exercise, as may any particular limb of the body. This sense is submitted, indeed, in some degree, to the guidance of reason; but it is a small stock which is required for this; even a less one than what we call common sense. State a moral case to a ploughman and a professor. The former will decide it as well, and often better than the latter, because he has not been led astray by artificial rules."

But this is true not only of farm boys and professors. It is equally true of judges. There is the remark attributed to Justice Samuel F. Miller, one of our great judges, appointed to the Supreme Court by Lincoln, "that a prime factor in shaping the law in our western states was ignorance; the first judges did not know enough to do the wrong thing, so they did the right thing." And there is the old story of the advice that Lord Chief Justice Mansfield gave the general who had been appointed governor of an island in the West Indies. The general came to Lord Mansfield for advice when he found that he was also to be the island's chief magistrate and he knew no law. "Nothing is easier," Lord Mansfield told him. "Consider what you think justice

requires and decide accordingly. But never give your reasons. For
your judgment will probably be right, but your reasons will certainly
be wrong."

"Judges know how to decide a good deal sooner than they know
why" is the way Justice Holmes put it. Holmes also said that judicial
decisions depend "on a judgment or intuition more subtle than any
articulate major premise." Why should we think that our capacity for
experience is restricted to our powers of expression?

What is the articulation of such intuitions but the natural element
in our law? It is the law that a lawyer finally appeals to when the
positive law runs out on his case. It is the law the judge must so often
at last turn to. The fact is, everybody who is at all seriously concerned
with the law—legislators, lawyers and judges, political scientists and
politicians, parties plaintiff and parties defendant—whether they were
aware of it or not, have believed in a natural law.

Natural law is the older. We need go no further back than Antigone, who, had she been born some five hundred years later, would
surely have been canonized as the patron saint of natural law. Antigone performed funeral rites over the body of her banished brother,
despite King Creon's edict that he be left unburied. She was brought
before Creon. She said:

> I cannot think your edict is so strong
> That it outruns the steadfast
> And unwritten laws of Heaven,
> Which live, not yesterday, nor yet today,
> But stand for ever;
> Those laws I would not break for any man.
> If I had left my mother's son unburied—
> I could not. But I can bear this.
> You think this foolish? Or are you the fool?

Antigone's faith in a higher law has run in a clear stream through the hearts of one generation after another down to the present. In 1947, the Reverend John J. Cavanaugh, the President of Notre Dame University, said, "The Natural Law is not an ideal; it is a reality. It is not a product of men's minds; it is a product of God's will. It is as real and binding as the statutes in the U.S. Code. It is not a mere ideal toward which all statutes and court decisions and systems of law should tend. The actuality is that any statute or court decision or system of law which does not conform to Natural Law simply has no valid binding force." There's a sparkle of light over the surface of this stream of faith, as it leaps from heart to heart, darkened from time to time as it runs aslant the shadow of divine might.

I know only enough about this, the purest kind of natural law, to ask questions. Is euthanasia to be regarded simply as murder? Is the wretched survivor of a suicide pact a common murderer? What about a doctor who declines to save the life of the mother by performing an abortion? Or about a society that makes abortions doubly dangerous by making them all illegal? What is wrong about contraception? May we have no more to say about our children than about our parents? Is it wrong for a man and wife to confirm and strengthen their love for each other by an act which has no ulterior purpose and no other consequence? Must children be bred only by the physical introduction of the father? Why may not a woman conceive by artificial insemination? If you can answer any of these questions without either invoking or denying a divine law, I cannot.

I do not know what to say. Will you sit in on the table talk of a great Elizabethan lawyer and scholar, John Selden? "I cannot fancy to myself what the Law of Nature means, but the Law of God. How should I know I ought not to steal, I ought not to commit adultery, unless somebody had told me so? 'Tis not because I think I ought not to do them, nor because you think I ought not; if so, our minds might change. Whence then comes the restraint? From a higher Power, nothing else can bind. I cannot bind myself, for I may untie myself again; nor an equal cannot bind me, for we may untie one another: it must be a superior Power, even God Almighty."

There is another kind of natural law, which we owe to Stoicism, the idealism of emperor and slave alike, Marcus Aurelius and Epictetus, now for many of us an unconfessed creed. The Stoics replaced God with Nature and supplanted Revelation with Reason. They preferred to worship at the sober shrine of Humanity. A man who had as much confidence in his fellow man as Thomas Jefferson could accept his Declaration of Independence with as much certitude as another man could avow Saint Thomas Aquinas and his *Summa*. "We hold these truths to be self-evident: that all men are created equal; that they are endowed by their Creator with certain unalienable rights; that among these are life, liberty, and the pursuit of happiness."

One thing to notice about this Declaration, which, as we know, was written by the three, Jefferson, Adams, and Franklin, and which, as Jefferson said, "was intended to be an expression of the American mind" or, as Adams put it, "contained no new ideas . . . a common-place compilation," is the primary place it gives to man. "Endowed," to be sure, "by their Creator," but the endowment consists in man's right to the pursuit of his own happiness. God is put further into the background than He would be today. As Perry Miller tells us, "the Founders were not what the majority of churchgoing Americans would ever consider religious, let alone Christian." They believed, Miller says, "that the Government should leave religion severely alone." (In his review of Norman Cousins' "In God We Trust, the Religious Beliefs and Ideas of the American Founding Fathers," in *The New York Times*, April 6, 1958.) And Jefferson's attitude toward the Deity is neatly reflected in a letter he wrote to Hartley in 1787: "I have no fear, but that the result of our experiment will be, that men may be trusted to govern themselves without a master. Could the

contrary of this be proved, I should conclude, either that there is no
God, or that He is a malevolent Being."

"The truth is," Carl Becker said, "that Locke, and the English
Whigs, and Jefferson and Rousseau even more so, had lost that sense
of intimate intercourse and familiar conversation with God which
religious men of the sixteenth and seventeenth centuries enjoyed.
Since the later seventeenth century, God had been withdrawing from
immediate contact with men, and had become, in proportion as he
receded into the dim distance, no more than the Final Cause, or Great
Contriver, or Prime Mover of the universe; and as such was conceived
as exerting his power and revealing his will indirectly through his
creation rather than directly by miraculous manifestation or through
inspired books. In the eighteenth century as never before, 'Nature' had
stepped in between man and God; so that there was no longer any
way to know God's will except by discovering the 'laws' of Nature,
which would doubtless be the laws of 'nature's god,' as Jefferson said.
'Why should I go in search of Moses to find out what God has said
to Jean Jacques Rousseau?' Why indeed, when the true revelation was
all about him in Nature, with sermons in stones, books in the running
brooks, and God in everything. The eighteenth century, seeking a
modified version of the original compact, had to find it in nature or
forever abandon the hope of finding it." (*The Declaration of Independence,* by Carl L. Becker, Vintage, 1958; p. 36.)

In the bright and dewy dawn of 1776, these self-evident inalienable
rights were summed up in the happy phrase "life, liberty, and the
pursuit of happiness." But as the day wore on toward noon, our First
Congress, drafting the Bill of Rights, changed "pursuit of happiness"
back to "property," which was how Locke had it. While we were
domesticating our continent, this was appropriate enough. Property
was what we worshiped, most of us, or as William James called it,
"the bitch-goddess, Success." But now we are no longer applauding
the cynical rhetoric of a Rufus Choate declaiming the Declaration of

Independence as "glittering generalities." We are almost ready to accept Emerson's angry reply, "No! Blazing ubiquities!" Property rights are no longer our only absolutes. The Great Certainties we now covet are no longer so provincial.

But why need natural law be such an absolute knave? For the noblest absolute is a harbor of refuge—to leeward, on a lee shore—as well as a port of embarkation.

It would be disastrous if our duty of obedience to the positive law were ever to become absolute. Remember the Nazis. Consider the Soviets. It is all very well to plead for a greater sense of obligation, a greater respect for authority, but we must beware of success. Soviet law stands on a premise of duty, as our law stands on rights. A sense of duty is a splendid virtue, but I had a sister-in-law who once remarked that doing your duty sometimes unfits you for doing anything else. Harold Berman has recently warned us that Soviet law conceives of man "rather as a youth, to be educated, disciplined, and protected or punished." This is not the way you and I regard each other.

Anyone who reads the *Antigone* should then read Plato's *Crito* and especially the colloquy between Socrates and the Laws of Athens. Crito was trying to persuade Socrates to break jail before it was too late. The Laws remonstrated, saying, "Are you trying to destroy us, Socrates? Do you imagine that a city can exist if its laws are nullified by its citizens? If you were not satisfied with us, you could have gone somewhere else. Do not take Crito's advice, but ours." And, as you know, Socrates took their advice, listening to them, he said, as he would to the pipes of the priests of the Goddess Cybele.

The great question is, How much of the *ought* which is in natural law to add to the *is* of positive law? It may be that Holmes did not offer us enough. "I do accept," Holmes wrote Laski, "a 'rough equation between isness and oughtness,' or rather I don't know anything about oughtness except Cromwell's—a few poor gentlemen have put their lives on it. You respect the rights of man—I don't, except those things a given crowd will fight for—which vary from religion to the price of a glass of beer."

This is not enough for those to whom the "stern daughter of the voice of God" is as absolute as Milton's Eve,

> So absolute she seems
> And in herself complete, so well to know
> Her own, that what she wills to do or say
> Seems wisest, virtuousest, discreetest, best.

No, there is no reason why our natural law should be absolute. Something less than divine, something short of universal, something less permanent than everlasting will serve our purpose. I ask you, Is perfection a virtue? Should we not be content with a natural law that gives us factors stable enough for us to treat them as if they were constants in the great equation of our justice?

This is a question each of us will answer for himself, depending in good part on how much we need or demand the superlative. This is the best explanation Holmes can offer of natural law. "It is not enough," he said, "for the knight of romance that you agree that his lady is a very nice girl—if you do not admit that she is the best that God ever made or will make, you must fight. There is in all men a demand for the superlative, so much so that the poor devil who has no other way of reaching it attains it by getting drunk. It seems to me that this demand is at the bottom of the philosopher's effort to prove that truth is absolute and of the jurist's search for criteria of universal validity which he collects under the head of Natural Law."

Another and less glorious reason for an absolute natural law is a sort of determinism. If natural law is unchangeable and everlasting, there is nothing we can do about it, except to sit back and listen. This is an attitude we often take. It is easy to believe that what we find hard to change cannot be changed, and what we can change only very

slowly is immovable. There is much to be said for this attitude on a
number of counts. Things often do work themselves out better when
they are not interfered with, but this attitude is, nevertheless, a stepping back from responsibility. We must not forget that it is only by
effort that we attain the inevitable as well as achieve the impossible.

I must clear up what I mean by "absolute." For here lies one great
difference between the old brands of natural law and the brand for
today which I am describing and advocating, and which is as relative
as I believe everything is, even the absolute itself having its own
degrees of more or less.

We are all tempted by an absolute. For some people, it is intellectual
thrift, saving thought and driving away doubt, emptying their mental
waste baskets and making everything as neat and tidy as can be. How
often a definition tends to become definitive! For others, it is a form
of intoxication and, as William James says somewhere in *The Varieties
of Religious Experience*, makes a man "one with the cosmos." For
some the absolute is "the Rock of Ages, cleft for me, Let me hide
myself in Thee," but there are the elect who find in it a sign of the
approach of God, and this can be as intoxicating as the cosmos. For
me the absolute is simply the result of rejecting or ignoring more and
more relevant considerations, until you get down to one, which turns
out to be, solipsistically, the absolute itself.

However, what's more to our purpose, an affection for the absolute
is a most unlawyerlike trait. For the chief pride and the greatest glory
of good lawyers is their skill in the art of the relevant. "Experts in
relevance," Felix Frankfurter calls them. Better than others, lawyers
know how to make a nice appraisal of the probable importance of the
various considerations that are pressed upon them and which they so
seldom have time to give their full attention to.

I wonder, by the way, whether it isn't this trait, the lawyer's proficiency in the art of the relevant, that makes lawyers so conservative
a race. First prudent, then cautious, and then, when they find them-

selves, like Balaam's ass, in a dilemma of conflicting considerations, conservative.

Nevertheless lawyers are subject to the same temptation as the rest of us. Possibly more so, because lawyers are on such familiar terms with generalities. I'll give you an example. Justice Douglas has said that his colleague, Justice Black, "has an ear finely tuned to facts and quite deaf to dogma and generalities." (*Yale Law Journal* for February 1956, the number devoted to Mr. Justice Black.) And yet Black sometimes falls victim to what lawyers call "a conclusive presumption," which is no more than a name for ignoring a confusing number of admittedly relevant considerations. Read what Milton Handler had to say about Black's attitude toward the Sherman Act in the October 1958 number of *The Record*.

"Although Mr. Justice Black recognizes that Section 1 of the Sherman Act has not received a literal interpretation and that the courts have read into its total prohibition the requirement that the restraint be unreasonable, he makes it abundantly clear that he has no sympathy for or belief in the rule of reason. After pointing out that 'there are certain agreements or practices which because of their pernicious effect on competition and lack of any redeeming virtue are conclusively presumed to be unreasonable and therefore illegal without elaborate inquiry as to the precise harm they have caused or the business excuse for their use,' he makes this revealing observation:

'This principle of *per se* unreasonableness not only makes the type of restraints which are proscribed by the Sherman Act more certain to the benefit of everyone concerned, but it also avoids the necessity for an incredibly complicated and prolonged economic investigation into the entire history of the industry involved, as well as related industries, in an effort to determine at large whether a particular restraint has been unreasonable—an inquiry so often wholly fruitless when undertaken.'

". . . The vice of this view, it seems to me, is that it moves in the direction of treating antitrust in terms of absolutes. To be sure, the businessman would like more certain guidance as to his vulnerability under the antitrust laws. But does he or anyone concerned with the proper functioning of the economy want certainty at the expense of unqualified prohibition of a wide variety of normal and useful business arrangements? The very nature of the conduct which antitrust seeks to control makes it inevitable that its legality will depend on a subtle weighing of various economic facts."

In all justice, this is unlike Black. Douglas is right in emphasizing Black's ear for facts and deafness to dogma. All you need to convince yourself of this is to look forward in this book to Black's insistence on the Court's reading the whole record in the criminal cases where the question is whether a confession was coerced. Take the *Payne* case, which I refer to on page 69, or Black's great opinion in the *Chambers* case (309 U.S. 227). There Black brought the Court as close to all the facts as he could get, even, were it possible, as close as the trial court, judge and jury, who saw and listened to the witnesses.

I am offering you, as you see, two extremes, neither commendable. It is in between that a lawyerlike skill in relevance leads to judicial salvation.

There are, nevertheless, some things in the law I think are the better for being treated as if they were absolutes. The verdict of juries, for one, in my opinion. The less lawyers know about juries, the better tribunal the jury is. I pay my respects to a judge. I stand in awe of a jury. There I am frankly obscurantist. But I have no such feelings about the Supreme Court, either as the prophet of our natural law or otherwise. The less mystery here, the better. Reason proved a sorry substitute for Revelation. Mysticism would fare no better; worse, in my opinion. For our natural law now, the one I am talking about, roots in the soil, in us. It needs sun, and a little rain, and a little manure now and then, but no other fertilizer. The most important thing about the natural law I am preaching is the fact that it is common knowledge. Otherwise it does not exist. So I take offense at its being revealed to some selected few and by them purveyed to us, as the Ten Commandments were.

You know how God revealed his Ten Commandments to the Israelites. Moses, and Aaron with him, went up to the top of Mount Sinai and there spoke with God and brought the Ten Commandments down. The people, by God's express desire, were not allowed to go up into the mount or touch the border of it. "Whosoever," He said, "touchest the mount shall surely be put to death." (Exodus, Chapter 19.) So the people "stood afar off. And they said unto Moses, Speak thou to us, and we will hear: but let not God speak with us, lest we die." (Exodus, 20: 19.)

"Moral codes," Alfred Whitehead warned us, "have suffered from the exaggerated claims made for them. The dogmatic fallacy has here done its worst. Each such code has been put out by a God on a mountain top, or by a Saint in a cave, or by a divine Despot on a throne, or, at the lowest, by ancestors with a wisdom beyond later question." (*Adventures of Ideas,* p. 374.) I should deny that such a code had any standing as natural law. I should call it an unauthorized kind of positive law, for it is imposed upon us.

Let me come at what I am trying to say from a different direction. Let me see what my meaning of absolute makes of those large phrases "due process," "equal protection," "freedom of speech," and any other of their kin. Hand has called them "admonitions of moderation" and "counsels of moderation." He has said that "we may read them as admonitory or hortatory, not definite enough to be guides on concrete occasions, prescribing no more than that temper of detachment, impartiality, and an absence of self-directed bias that is the whole content of justice." Then, in the next sentence but one, Hand calls them "commands, for indubitably they are."

I reconcile these two statements "admonition" versus "command" as opposite ends of a gamut of meanings: at one end, admonitions and counsels of moderation; at the other end, commands.

A *command* must be definite, specific. Otherwise, how are you going to *obey* it? Now work up the scale toward the absolute, into greater and greater degrees of generality, where obedience acquires a greater and greater amount of independent and individual judgment, and a command turns into an admonition. The difficulty is that there is nothing to indicate where you are to stop, where obedience becomes a matter of voluntary compliance as the command turns into an admonition, where a man can sit down and rest the feet of his obedience. There's an absolute in each of these phrases for everyone who shrinks from matters of degree and does not know or want to decide for himself where he shall stop. So he goes on to the top, where he finds the absolute he then knows he was seeking.

It need not be so. I was walking down Water Street in Stonington the other day to get the Sunday papers. I stopped to read a chalked inscription on a large flagstone in the sidewalk, just to one side of a hopscotch diagram. "Rules," it read, and then underneath:

1. No cheating.
2.
3.

Only Rule 1 was filled in. The young lady with the piece of chalk, the Constitutional Convention of 1787, and the Thirty-ninth Congress, all had the same idea, and it was a good one.

There is another dimension to the absolute that I find hard to take seriously, the dimension of time—or, rather, its denial, for your complete absolutist defies time, claiming that his code is not only everlasting but unchanging. I can no more believe this than think that I can step twice into the same river. Laws no more stagnate than societies, though some societies move very slowly—ant colonies, coral atolls, and mountain ranges. It is only when you measure the speed of change against the life span or the active career of an individual that a law can possibly be regarded as even comparatively constant. The shorter sighted we are, the more absolute we may safely dare to be, for the change may then be negligible, as it is on a short segment of a curve. The notion that natural law is the same yesterday, today, and forever is only something cherished by the more satisfied and complacent of us. I do not mean the reactionaries. They want more change than anybody—backward.

So we must think of the natural law which the courts apply as provisional and tentative. This, I think, is why courts so often make their opinions sound so assertive and dogmatic. They are whistling up their courage. For they are anxiously aware of the carefully appraised doubts and the equally carefully discounted certitudes from which their decision finally emerged. They embellish it with a verity or two, because they know that it is as mundane and human as they are or we are. The only thing they know for sure is that this is the best they can do. If they raise their voice, it is as much to encourage themselves as it is to convince us. And no wonder! How much less courage it would take, had their decision indeed been firmly set on some eternal verity! How much more admirable their courage than a faith which would make it unnecessary!

IV

N ow I OFFER you a prime example of this natural-law component that I have been trying to describe. It is, of course, the great decision on racial segregation of May 17, 1954, in which the Supreme Court held that "segregation in public schools deprives these plaintiffs of the equal protection of the laws," because "the opportunity of an education, where the state has undertaken to provide it, is a right which must be made available to all on equal terms." The Justices were telling us again what Lincoln told us a hundred years ago in his debate with Douglas. The Founders, he said, "defined with tolerable distinctness in what respects they did consider all men created equal—equal in 'certain inalienable rights, among which are life, liberty, and the pursuit of happiness.' This they said, and this meant, to set up a standard maxim for free society, which could be familiar to all, and revered by all; constantly looked to, constantly labored for, and even though never perfectly attained, constantly approximated, and thereby constantly spreading and deepening its influence, and augmenting the happiness and value of life to all people of all colors everywhere."

Natural law? Indeed it is. No longer as absolute as Jefferson would like to see it, but a modern, practicable, and no less idealistic brand. Our Supreme Court recognizes no absolutes. Chief Justice Fred Vinson aroused all devout dogmatists when he said, in the *Dennis* case, "Nothing is more certain in modern society than the principle that there are no absolutes, that a name, a phrase, a standard, has meaning only when

associated with the considerations which gave birth to the nomencla-
ture." (341 U.S. at 508.)

I ask you to take note of the field marks. To begin with, the large
generality of the constitutional language on which the Court relied,
"due process of law" and "the equal protection of the laws." What's
more, the Court relied on either *and* both, on due process of law in
the case which came up from a state, on equal protection in the
District of Columbia case. The Court said, "The two phrases are not
mutually exclusive." (*Bolling* v. *Sharpe,* 347 U.S. 497.) But the unmistakable field mark lies in the futile way the decision was enforced
or, rather, unenforced.

This is the grievous lesson of Little Rock. The unmistakable sign of
natural law is the ineffectiveness of force. Positive law relies on the
compulsion of a penalty, and when this is not effective, force; and no
harm is done. But when we see that compulsion is ineffective, or when
it defeats, instead of serves, its purpose, or when it even denatures
what it compels us to do, we know we are dealing with a large component of natural law.

From May 17, 1954, when the Supreme Court made its decision, to
September 1957, when President Eisenhower sent the 101st Airborne
Infantry to Little Rock, the President stood firmly behind the Court's
decree, but he did nothing except urge Congress to set up a bipartisan
commission. When nineteen Senators and eighty-one Representatives,
in March 1956, issued a manifesto attacking the Court and coming so
close to defying its decree that the two national leaders in the Democratic party, Speaker Sam Rayburn and Senator Lyndon Johnson, were
excused from signing it, the President said, "We must be patient without being complacent." He continued to stand on his respect for Law,
as if there were nothing for him to do, as if, indeed, the enforcement
of the Court's decree were wholly judicial business, until he was
surprised and dismayed to find that the situation in Little Rock left

him no choice but to enforce the Court's decision in the worst way possible, by force of what we may fairly call the secular arm.

The desegregation of our schools is almost wholly a matter of persuasion, of which there are a number of varieties, from exhortation to reluctant dollars. Force is at most but seasoning to this dish. President Eisenhower's attitude toward law is curiously like the attitude Holmes advised the law students to take as the best way to learn it. Those gentlemen who drafted the Constitution were more familiar with natural law than we are, and I think that the graceful phrase they chose for the President's duty to execute the laws sprang from their knowledge of the way natural law must be enforced. Turn the words over on your tongue: "he shall take Care that the Laws be faithfully executed."

It is a lovely phrase, and sometimes I wonder whether Gouverneur Morris, who was the chairman of the Convention's Committee on Style, should not be rated high among the lights in our literary history. And it is a demanding phrase, demanding more of the President than Eisenhower gave it. He acted like the good citizen he is, but not like a good President, for he did not "take Care that the Laws be faithfully executed," and so the best he could do, when the time came, was to be nothing more than a Commander in Chief. And why? Because he did not know the difference between positive law and natural law.

What should Eisenhower have done? What should he now be doing? I quote a paragraph that appeared in the *Wall Street Journal* in the spring of 1958. "It avails nothing to have good programs if you cannot persuade people they are good and rally support for them. And that is rarely done by abstract argument. It requires a combination of personal contact, persuasion, cajolery, returning support for support given, rewards where available and sometimes retribution where possible. In short, politics."

Not to speak of economics. Are we about to see our fine moral principles come true for mercenary reasons, as chambers of commerce come to see that racial discrimination is bad for business, sooner possibly than the churches become converted to Christian doctrine? Truly a triumph of reason over revelation. Neither churches nor chambers of commerce, I may add, will be the first. I am in no position to list the standing of the teams in this moral league, but I believe baseball leads, with the Dodgers and Jackie Robinson. And is not the Roman Catholic Church in the upper division, and the Southern Baptists in the cellar? Am I wrong that the universities and colleges, except for Vanderbilt, are still behind professional sport and the labor unions? And what shall we say for evangelism? Has Billy Graham yet risen to meet Reinhold Niebuhr's challenge to preach a sermon against segregation? (*The Christian Century*, August 8, 1956.) What a pity!

To a meticulous mind, every case is unique, and so an equal justice becomes impossible, or for that matter any justice within the reach of human adjudication. But sometimes we do get a case that is without precedent, and then we have nothing but natural law to turn to. Such a case came to the Court in 1947. (*Louisiana* v. *Resweber*, 329 U.S. 459.) The facts were these:

Willie Francis was convicted of murder in the Louisiana courts and sentenced to death by electrocution. When the executioner threw the switch, through some mechanical difficulty the machine did not work and Willie was not killed. The Governor reprieved him, and then issued a new death warrant. Willie then claimed that another attempt would be a "cruel and unusual punishment" forbidden by the Eighth and the Fourteenth Amendments and applied for a writ of certiorari, which was granted, and his execution was stayed until the Court could decide.

An affidavit by the attending chaplain gives you some idea of what happened. He reported:

"After Willie was strapped to the chair the Sheriff of St. Martin Parish asked him if he had anything to say about anything, and he said nothing. Then the hood was placed before his eyes. Then the officials in charge of the electrocution were adjusting the mechanisms, and when the needle of the meter registered to a certain point on the dial, the electrocutioner pulled down on the switch and at the same time said, 'Goodbye, Willie.' At that very moment, Willie Francis' lips puffed out and his body squirmed and tensed and he jumped so that the chair rocked on the floor. Then the condemned man said, 'Take it off. Let me breathe.' Then the switch was turned off. Then some of the men left, and a few minutes after the Sheriff of St. Martin Parish, Mr. E. L. Resweber, came in and announced that the governor had granted the condemned man a reprieve."

The record before the Court had this affidavit, and it had also a statement by the sheriff of a neighboring parish, not named, who accompanied Willie from the chair. This sheriff stated that Willie told him, on leaving the chair, "that the electric current had 'tickled him.' " But the record before the Court did not have—more's the pity—the story from Willie himself. A newspaper reporter interviewed Willie afterward, and Willie told him what really happened. Here it is, as published in the New York *Herald Tribune*:

"Whatever did happen, Willie Francis did not die. Some newspaper correspondents have played upon the word 'tickled' as the sensation experienced by the friendless black boy as he looked over Jordan. But Willie Francis, telling it better than any other human being of our time, has described the sensation of dying but not quite achieving death.

" 'You feel like you got a mouthful of cold peanut butter and you see little blue and pink and green speckles in front of your eyes, the kind that shines in a rooster's tail. All I could think was Willie, you're going out'n this world,' he continued to a reporter who had both a heart and the poetic imagination to write down Willie's words just as they fell from his lips.

" 'They begun to strap me against the chair and everything begun to look dazey in the room. It was like the white folks watching was on a big swing and they swung away-y-y back and then right up close to me where I could hear their breathing. I didn't think of my whole life like at the picture show, just Willie, you're going out'n this world in this bad chair. Sometimes I thought it so loud it hurt my head, and when they put the black bag over my head I was all locked up inside the bag with the loud thinking.'

"And then Willie Francis told the color of death: 'Some folks say it's gold; some say it's white as hominy grits. I reckon it's black. I ought to know, I been mighty close.'

"The steel cap by now had been applied and the electrodes fastened as tight as Willie's skinny, undernourished legs would allow. The 'electric man' said, 'Goodbye, Willie,' but Willie was too frightened to answer.

" 'He could have been putting me on a bus for New Orleans the way he said it, and I tried to say goodbye but my tongue got stuck in the peanut butter, and I felt a burning in my head and my left leg and I jumped against the straps. When the straps kept cutting me I hoped I was alive and I asked the electric man to let me breathe.' "

Here, surely, was the unique case, the case without precedent, which would drive the most legalistic lawyer to natural law. Let's see.

Four of the Justices found nothing in what had taken place that amounted, they said, to "cruel and unusual punishment in the constitutional sense. . . . Petitioner's suggestion is that because he once underwent the psychological strain of preparation for electrocution, now to require him to undergo this preparation again subjects him to a lingering or cruel and unusual punishment. Even the fact that petitioner has already been subjected to a current of electricity does not make his subsequent execution any more cruel in the constitutional sense than any other execution. The cruelty against which the Constitution protects a convicted man is cruelty inherent in the method of punishment, not the necessary suffering involved in any method employed to extinguish life humanely. The fact that an unforeseeable accident prevented the prompt consummation of the sentence cannot, it seems to us, add an element of cruelty to a subsequent execution. There is no purpose to inflict unnecessary pain nor any unnecessary pain involved in the proposed execution. The situation of the unfortunate victim of this accident is just as though he had suffered the identical amount of mental anguish and physical pain in any other occurrence, such as, for example, a fire in the cell block. We cannot agree that the hardship imposed upon the petitioner rises to that level of hardship denounced as denial of due process because of cruelty."

Briefly put, an accident may well be unusual, but it cannot be cruel. No natural law here. Only four sound lawyers scrutinizing a phrase.

Four Justices took it less calmly. They said:

"Taking human life by unnecessarily cruel means shocks the most fundamental instincts of civilized man. It should not be possible under the constitutional procedure of a self-governing people. Abhorrence of the cruelty of ancient forms of capital punishment has increased steadily until, today, some states have prohibited capital punishment altogether. It is unthinkable that any state legislature in modern times would enact a statute expressly authorizing capital punishment by repeated applications of an electric current separated by intervals of days or hours until finally death shall result. . . .

"In determining whether the proposed procedure is unconstitutional, we must measure it against a lawful electrocution. The contrast is that between instantaneous death and death by installments—caused by electric shocks administered after one or more intervening periods of complete consciousness of the victim. . . .

"The all-important consideration is that the execution shall be so instantaneous and substantially painless that the punishment shall be reduced, as nearly as possible, to no more than that of death itself. Electrocution has been approved only in a form that eliminates suffering.

"The Louisiana statute makes this clear. It provides that:

Every sentence of death imposed in this State shall be by electrocution—that is, causing to pass through the body of the person
convicted a current of electricity of sufficient intensity to cause
death, and the application and continuance of such current through
the body of the person convicted until such person is dead. . . .
(La. Code of Criminal Procedure, 1928, Act No. 2, Art. 569, as
amended by § 1, Act No. 14, 1940.)

"It does not provide for electrocution by interrupted or repeated
applications of electric current at intervals of several days or even
minutes. It does not provide for the application of electric current of
an intensity less than that sufficient to cause death. It prescribes expressly and solely for the application of a current of sufficient intensity
to cause death and for the *continuance* of that application until death
results. Prescribing capital punishment, it should be construed strictly.
There can be no implied provision for a second, third or multiple application of the current. There is no statutory or judicial precedent
upholding a delayed process of electrocution."

Here you observe the application of natural law, "the most fundamental instincts of civilized man. . . . It is unthinkable that any
state legislature in modern times . . ."

The ninth Justice, Felix Frankfurter, wished he could, but he could
not. For he knew the difference between a man's own personal opinion
and that consensus of social opinion which is natural law. Frankfurter said:

"I cannot bring myself to believe that for Louisiana to leave to executive clemency, rather than to require, mitigation of a sentence of
death duly pronounced upon conviction for murder because a first
attempt to carry it out was an innocent misadventure, offends a principle of justice 'rooted in the traditions and conscience of our people.'
Short of the compulsion of such a principle, this Court must abstain
from interference with State action no matter how strong one's per-

sonal feeling of revulsion against a State's insistence on its pound of flesh. One must be on guard against finding in personal disapproval a reflection of more or less prevailing condemnation. Strongly drawn as I am to some of the sentiments expressed by my brother Burton, I cannot rid myself of the conviction that were I to hold that Louisiana would transgress the Due Process Clause if the State were allowed, in the precise circumstances before us, to carry out the death sentence, I would be enforcing my private view rather than that consensus of society's opinion which, for purposes of due process, is the standard enjoined by the Constitution."

So Willie's appeal failed. The State Pardon Board refused to act. The Governor refused to act. A second appeal to the Court failed. So the portable electric chair was set up again in the little jail house in St. Martinville. The power truck drove up again. And this time Willie Francis got all the way across the river on February 11, 1947. (Letter from Willie's attorney, now Judge J. Skelly Wright of the U.S. District Court for the Southern District of Louisiana, December 29, 1958.)

Racial desegregation in our schools and cruelty in punishment are too obviously cases of natural law for demonstration purposes. I want to make it quite clear that the natural-law component crops up in places less emotional and less sensational. Take for another prime example the jurisdiction of state courts in civil cases.

I was brought up in law school on the case of *Pennoyer* v. *Neff* (95 U.S. 714), which held the field of doctrine from 1877 to 1945. This doctrine was, briefly: "The foundation of jurisdiction is physical power." (*McDonald* v. *Mabee*, 243 U.S. 90.) A state court had no jurisdiction over an individual unless he was physically present in the state or actually resident there, nor over a foreign corporation unless it either consented or at least was doing business in the state. These were good hardheaded criteria, and intellectually satisfying.

Then in 1945 came a case in which the Court put such crass considerations behind it and held that the question whether a state court had jurisdiction in a civil case over a nonresident individual or a foreign corporation depended on "traditional notions of fair play and substantial justice." (*International Shoe Co.* v. *Washington,* 326 U.S. 310; see *McGee* v. *International Life Insurance Co.,* 355 U.S. 220.) The fact is, I don't know where a lawyer would be safe from the fallout of natural law. The Internal Revenue Code? The place is full of it.

V

I come now to the display in my show window. I chose it because here in a series of cases the Justices carried on a running argument about natural law, Hugo Black, for a minority of the Court, charging that the majority were practicing natural law, Frankfurter defending the majority and declaring that due process of law was not to be derided as a revival of "natural law." In these cases, the Court was engaged in applying the Fourteenth Amendment to the States: "Nor shall any State deprive any person of life, liberty, or property without due process of law; nor deny to any person within its jurisdiction the equal protection of the laws," which, as you know, is the bite of the Fourteenth Amendment.

Fifty years ago, our Supreme Court concluded, in the *Twining* case, that New Jersey could constitutionally compel a man to testify against himself. This, the Court held, was due process of law, despite the provision in the Bill of Rights which forbids the Federal Government to do it. Just because it is in the Bill of Rights does not necessarily make it "an essential element of due process of law. If that were so, the procedure of the first half of the seventeenth century would be fastened upon the American jurisprudence like a strait jacket, only to be unloosed by constitutional amendment." (211 U.S. 78.)

Thirty years later, in 1937, the question arose whether a State could try a man twice for the same offense. Under the Bill of Rights, no person, in the courts of the United States, shall "be subject for the

same offense to be twice put in jeopardy of life and limb." Again the
Court refused to apply the Bill of Rights to a State. Connecticut could
try a man twice, if it chose to. Justice Cardozo explained how the
Court went about it. Only such rights, he said, as were "implicit in
the concept of ordered liberty" applied to the States. Freedom of
thought and speech, yes. "Of that freedom," he said, "one may say that
it is the matrix, the indispensable condition, of nearly every other
form of freedom." Of the other provisions in the Bill of Rights,
Cardozo said that the question must always be: Is it one of those
"fundamental principles of liberty and justice which lie at the base
of all our civil and political institutions?" (*Palko* v. *Connecticut*, 302
U.S. 319.)

All the Court had to go on was the phrase in the Fourteenth Amendment "life, liberty, and property, without due process of law," which,
as we have seen, was the phrase into which our First Congress revised
Jeffersonian Natural Law. But had Cardozo's phrase done more than
substitute one unknown quantity for another in the equation of
justice? This is how it looked to some of the Justices when the question next came up in 1947. Black was their spokesman:

"I cannot consider the Bill of Rights to be an outworn eighteenth-
century strait jacket as the Twining opinion did. Its provisions may
be thought outdated abstractions by some. And it is true that they
were designed to meet ancient evils. But they are the same kind of
human evils that have emerged from century to century wherever
excessive power is sought by the few at the expense of the many. . . .
I fear to see the consequences of the Court's practice of substituting
its own concepts of decency and fundamental justice for the language
of the Bill of Rights as its point of departure in interpreting and enforcing that Bill of Rights.

"Conceding the possibility that this Court is now wise enough to
improve on the Bill of Rights by substituting natural-law concepts for
the Bill of Rights, I think the possibility is entirely too speculative to

agree to take that course. I would therefore hold in this case that the full protection of the Fifth Amendment's proscription against compelled testimony must be afforded by California. . . .

"It must be conceded, of course, that the natural-law-due-process formula, which the Court today reaffirms, has been interpreted to limit substantially this Court's power to prevent state violation of the individual civil liberties guaranteed by the Bill of Rights. But this formula also has been used in the past and can be used in the future to license this Court, in considering regulatory legislation, to roam at large in the broad expanses of policy and morals and to trespass, all too freely, on the legislative domain of the States as well as the Federal Government. . . .

"To pass upon the Constitutionality of the statutes by looking to the particular standards enumerated in the Bill of Rights and other parts of the Constitution is one thing; to invalidate statutes because of application of 'natural law' deemed to be above and undefined by the Constitution is another. In the one instance, courts proceeding within clearly marked constitutional boundaries seek to execute policies written into the Constitution; in the other, they roam at will in the limitless area of their own beliefs as to reasonableness and actually select policies, a responsibility which the Constitution entrusts to the legislative representatives of the people." (Black and Douglas dissenting in *Adamson* v. *California,* 332 U.S. 46; 1947.)

This was in 1947. Five years later, in 1952, the dispute was still open, and Frankfurter, speaking for the Court, replied.

Frankfurter denied with some vehemence that this was natural law, and I will give you the heart of what he said. "Due process of law thus conceived," Frankfurter said, "is not to be derided as a resort to a revival of 'natural law.' . . . The faculties of the Due Process Clause may be indefinite and vague, but the mode of their ascertainment is not self-willed. In each case 'due process of law' requires an evaluation based on a disinterested inquiry pursued in the spirit of science, on a balanced order of facts exactly and fairly stated, on the detached consideration of conflicting claims, on a judgment not *ad hoc* and episodic but duly mindful of reconciling the needs both of continuity and change in a progressive society." (*Rochin* v. *California,* 342 U.S. 165.)

No, this is not, I agree, "a revival of 'natural law,'" but is not what Frankfurter is here describing just such a modern version as I have been expounding and proposing as a substitute?

Frankfurter said more, but this more I am going to let Black summarize for you in his rejoinder.

Black rejoined: "What the majority hold is that the Due Process Clause empowers this Court to nullify any state law if its application 'shocks the conscience,' offends 'a sense of justice,' or runs counter to the 'decencies of civilized conduct.' The majority emphasize that these statements do not refer to their own consciences or to their senses of justice and decency. For we are told that 'we may not draw on our merely personal and private notions'; our judgment must be grounded on 'considerations deeply rooted in reason and in the compelling traditions of the legal profession.' We are further admonished to measure the validity of state practices, not by our reason, or by the traditions of the legal profession, but by 'the community's sense of fair play and decency'; by the 'traditions and conscience of our people'; or by 'those canons of decency and fairness which express the notions of justice of English-speaking peoples.' These canons are made necessary, it is said, because of 'interests of society pushing in opposite directions.' . . .

"What paralyzing role this same philosophy will play in the future economic affairs of this country is impossible to predict. Of even graver concern, however, is the use of the philosophy to nullify the Bill of Rights. I long ago concluded that the accordionlike qualities of this philosophy must inevitably imperil all the individual liberty safeguards specifically enumerated in the Bill of Rights. Reflection and recent decisions of this Court sanctioning abridgment of the freedom of speech and press have strengthened this conclusion." (*Rochin* v. *California*, 342 U.S. 165.)

Before we get any further into this, let me make sure we know what we are dealing with. It is the Fourteenth Amendment itself and in its own right, and not as a vehicle for any of the provisions in the Bill of Rights. Black made this mistake. He thought it was implicit in Cardozo's opinion in the Palko case that some of the provisions of the Bill of Rights applied to the States "by their very terms." (*Adamson*, 332 U.S. at 85.) Justice Robert H. Jackson made the same mistake in his opinion in the *Barnette* case (319 U.S. at 639) and later corrected himself. In *Beauharnais* v. *Illinois* (343 U.S. 250 at 288), Jackson said he was convinced "that the Fourteenth Amendment did not 'incorporate' the First, that the powers of Congress and of the States over this subject are not of the same dimensions, and that because Congress probably could not enact this law [making group libel a crime] it does not follow that the States may not." And Jackson went on to quote Holmes and Brandeis to the same effect "as the wise and historically correct view of the Fourteenth Amendment." Holmes said, in the *Gitlow* case (268 U.S. at 672), "The general principles of free speech, it seems to me, must be taken to be included in the Fourteenth Amendment, in view of the scope that has been given to the word *liberty* as there used, although perhaps it may be accepted with a somewhat larger latitude of interpretation than is allowed to Congress by the sweeping language that governs or ought to govern the laws of the United States." And recently Harlan came to the same conclusion about obscene publications. (*Roth* v. *U.S.*, 354 U.S. 476 at 503.)

No, the Fourteenth Amendment speaks for itself. It is not a John Alden speaking for a Myles Standish. The Court, then, as I see it, is quite simply articulating a modern code of natural law for the state courts.

What do you say? Which do you choose? This modern judicial version? Or the first eight Amendments, our Bill of Rights?

Before you make up your mind, let me say a word about Black.

VI

I DON'T THINK we can understand these dissenting opinions of Black
and his preference for the Bill of Rights over the simple Due
Process of the Fourteenth Amendment without some understanding
of Black himself. These dissents are eloquent, even emotional, as an
intellectual effort so often does well to be. What is it, then, about
Black that lies behind and beneath his opinions? I think I know. It is
the Natural Law of the Declaration of Independence. I think I can
prove this.

Black is a child of the Enlightenment, and what Kant said about the
Age of Enlightenment is true of Black. "Have the courage," Kant said,
"to avail yourself of your own understanding—that is the motto of the
Enlightenment." And, in particular, as an American, Black is the
spiritual descendant and heir of Thomas Jefferson. Twenty years ago,
after Black's first term of court, I wrote an article about him in the
Atlantic Monthly. He had then been only one year on the Court and
ten in the Senate. I called him a legislator among judges. I said that he
had the attitude of the artist toward the critic and that he had an
understanding and an appreciation of the legislator's pride of craft.
Now he has been twenty years a judge, and there is more to go on.

Black once told the Senate that he had read "a great deal of Thomas
Jefferson's philosophy." He had been exposed to a Jeffersonian
philosophy at an early age, and we may surmise that he was following
up a youthful enthusiasm. For, in 1896, when Black was ten, William

Jennings Bryan was bringing the Populist program into the Democratic party. The Democrats of Clay County in Alabama, where
Black was brought up, backed Bryan as the Democratic-Populist
candidate. Thus, as John P. Frank says in his book, *Mr. Justice Black,*
Black "became absolutely saturated with the essential conception of the
Populist philosophy—that the people had the right through their
government to improve the condition of their daily lives." (*Mr.
Justice Black,* by John P. Frank, Knopf, 1949; pp. 10-12.) Thence it
was an easy and obvious ascent to the New Deal; and thence also
back to Jefferson, for Populism, at any rate as it was proclaimed and
preached by Bryan, was thoroughly Jeffersonian. It is all too easy
and very much mistaken to think of Bryan as no more than an advocate of Free Silver and Fundamentalism.

"Despite occasional lapses—" I quote Edward R. Lewis—"Bryan
was at heart an individualist of the old Jeffersonian school. In fact, the
root of Bryan's political philosophy is Thomas Jefferson. . . . The
Populists, Turner says, were the spiritual descendants, in a long line, of
the Levellers and sectaries of Cromwell's army, the minutemen of the
Revolution, the Abolitionist, the Granger, who 'saw the sharp contrast
between their traditional idea of America as the land of opportunity,
the land of the self-made man, free from class distinctions and from
the power of wealth, and the existing America, so unlike the earlier
ideal.' " (*A History of American Political Thought,* by Edward R.
Lewis, Macmillan, 1937; pp. 320, 304-5.)

Black's exaltation of the First Amendment is the most trenchant
parallel with Jefferson. In 1955, Black's daughter was graduated from
Swarthmore, and he gave the commencement address, and he said,
"We desperately need today a new Jefferson and a new baptism in
his sane and sound faith in complete freedom to think, speak, and
write." And he went on, "In my judgment, the very heart of the Bill
of Rights is the First Amendment. Unless people can freely exercise
those liberties, without loss of good name, job, property, liberty or

life, a good society cannot exist. That is my faith. I believe that without the liberties of that Amendment your commencement here would be a very sad one indeed—if you had any. Why should you be here to learn how to think and how to challenge if it should be against the law to think and to challenge?"

But Black is most eloquent when there is something to be done as well as something to be said. Words to him spell action as well as express thought. In the *Yates* case, in 1957, the appeal of fourteen Communists convicted of subversive teaching, Black said, "I believe that the First Amendment forbids Congress to punish people for talking about public affairs, whether or not such discussion incites to action, legal or illegal." And Black added, "As the Virginia Assembly said in 1785, in its Statute for Religious Liberty, written by Thomas Jefferson, it is time enough, for the rightful purposes of civil government, for its officers to interfere when principles break out into overt acts against peace and good order. . . ." (*Yates* v. *U.S.*, 354 U.S. 298.)

Six years before that, in the *Dennis* case, when the leaders of the Communist party were convicted, Black had expressed his belief that Holmes' and Brandeis' test of free speech was the beginning, not the end, of wisdom. Black said, "At least as to speech in the realm of public matters, I believe that the clear and present danger test does not mark the furthermost constitutional boundaries of protected expression but does no more than recognize a minimum compulsion of the Bill of Rights." (*Dennis* v. *U.S.*, 341 at 494; June 1951.)

It is here, on free thought and free speech, that Black and Jefferson speak indistinguishably.

In June 1958, California required a loyalty oath of honorably discharged veterans and of churches. They had to swear to their loyalty before they could get their respective property tax exemptions. Both refused to take that or any test oath. The First Unitarian Church of Los Angeles stated:

"The principles, moral and religious, of the First Unitarian Church of Los Angeles compel it, its members, officers, and minister, as a matter of deepest conscience, belief, and conviction, to deny power in the state to compel acceptance by it or any other church of this or any other oath of coerced affirmation as to church doctrine, advocacy, or beliefs."

The Court held the requirement of an oath unconstitutional in both cases. (*Speiser* v. *Randall* and *First Unitarian Church* v. *Los Angeles,* 357 U.S. 513 and 545.) Black and Douglas concurred, in separate opinions. Black said:

"The mere fact that California attempts to exact this ill-concealed penalty from individuals and churches and that its validity has to be considered in this Court only emphasizes how dangerously far we have departed from the fundamental principles of freedom declared in the First Amendment. We should never forget that the freedoms secured by that Amendment—Speech, Press, Religion, Petition, and Assembly—are absolutely indispensable for the preservation of a free society in which government is based upon the consent of an informed citizenry and is dedicated to the protection of the rights of all, even the most despised minorities.

"This case offers just another example of a wide-scale effort by government in this country to impose penalties and disabilities on everyone who is or is suspected of being a 'Communist' or who is not ready at all times and all places to swear his loyalty to State and Nation. Government employees, lawyers, doctors, teachers, pharmacists, veterinarians, subway conductors, industrial workers, and a multitude of others have been denied an opportunity to work at their trade or profession for these reasons. Here a tax is levied unless the taxpayer makes an oath that he does not and will not in the future advocate certain things; in Ohio those without jobs have been denied unemployment insurance unless they are willing to swear that they do not hold specific views; and Congress has even attempted to deny public housing to needy families unless they first demonstrate their loyalty. These are merely random samples; I will not take time here to refer to innumerable others, such as oaths for hunters and fishermen, wrestlers and boxers and junk dealers.

"I am convinced that this whole business of penalizing people because of their views and expressions concerning government is hopelessly repugnant to the principles of freedom upon which this Nation was founded and which have helped to make it the greatest in the world. As stated in prior cases, I believe 'that the First Amendment grants an absolute right to believe in any governmental system, [to] discuss all governmental affairs, and [to] argue for desired changes in the existing order. This freedom is too dangerous for bad, tyrannical governments to permit. But those who wrote and adopted our First Amendment weighed those dangers against the dangers of censorship and deliberately chose the First Amendment's unequivocal command that freedom of assembly, petition, speech, and press shall not be abridged. I happen to believe this was a wise choice and that our free way of life enlists such respect and love that our Nation cannot be imperiled by mere talk.'

"Loyalty oaths, as well as other contemporary 'security measures,' tend to stifle all forms of unorthodox or unpopular thinking or expression—the kind of thought and expression which has played such a vital and beneficial role in the history of this Nation. The result is a stultifying conformity which in the end may well turn out to be more destructive to our free society than foreign agents could ever hope to be. The course which we have been following the last decade is not the course of a strong, free, secure people, but that of the frightened, the insecure, the intolerant. I am certain that loyalty to the United States can never be secured by the endless proliferation of 'loyalty' oaths; loyalty must arise spontaneously from the hearts of people who love their country and respect their government. I also adhere to the proposition that the 'First Amendment provides the only kind of security system that can preserve a free government—one that leaves the way wide open for people to favor, discuss, advocate, or incite causes and doctrines however obnoxious and antagonistic such views may be to the rest of us.' "

I like calling the First Amendment a "security system." That's pure Jefferson. It is likewise Benjamin Franklin, for it was Poor Richard who put it, characteristically, into a paradox: "The way to be safe is never to be secure."

I think I can sum up Black's and Jefferson's joint preference for the First Amendment by suggesting that just as Jefferson replaced Locke's "property" with "the pursuit of happiness" in the Declaration of Independence, which the post-revolutionary generation restored in the Constitution, so Black would now again make the pursuit of happiness the linchpin of our well-being.

There is opposition to this "Firstness of the First Amendment," as Edmond Cahn calls it (*Yale Law Journal* for February 1956, an issue in honor of Black), this preferred constitutional position of free speech, which magnetizes Black as powerfully as it did Jefferson, and Cardozo too, for that matter, as we have seen in his opinion in the *Palko* case. Hand "can see no more persuasive reason for supposing that a legislature is *a priori* less qualified to choose between 'personal' than between economic values."

Frankfurter objects to the preference from the same judicial point of view. "Our power does not vary according to the particular provision of the Bill of Rights which is invoked. The right not to have property taken without just compensation has, so far as the scope of judicial power is concerned, the same constitutional dignity as the right to be protected against unreasonable searches and seizures, and the latter has no less claim than freedom of the press or freedom of speech or religious freedom. In no instance is this Court the primary protector of the particular liberty that is invoked." (*Board of Education* v. *Barnette*, 319 U.S. at 648.)

It is fair, indeed more than fair, for a legislature to prefer things
of the spirit to more material needs, but even a legislature must not be
misled by Cahn's quip. It is the necessities that come first, our job,
our home, our property, enough to send the girl as well as the boy to
college. Liberties of the mind and tongue and pen, we need them less
and prize them the more. Freedom of expression may be—and is—
"the matrix, the indispensable condition" of all the other freedoms,
as Cardozo said, but what comes first, and has top priority, is enough
to eat and drink, a place to work, another to sleep, and some reason
to hope that your children will be off to a better start than either of
you were. These are "property," if you please, and they are not to
be put in second place. To be sure, men may hold some things better
and other things worse. But, to manhandle Heraclitus, the Court, like
a god, ought to hold all these things fair.

But if we must rank these rights, let us rank them, not by favor,
like kisses, but by practical political considerations. If the Court is to
go in for statesmanship, the Court must learn how to play politics,
the art of the possible as well as the noble. See if you don't agree with
the following axioms (which I take from an article I wrote in the
Wisconsin Law Review for March 1944) :

When the statute, order, regulation, or whatever it is that the
Court is passing an opinion on is not the result of the democratic
process, let the Court drop all pretense at self-restraint or humility
and do what it can for us. This is the basis on which the Court acts
on a state's regulation of interstate commerce or a state's tax on
interstate commerce when the burden falls principally on the citizens
of *another* state. (303 U.S. at 185; 309 U.S. at 46; 314 U.S. at 400-1.)
Justice James Byrnes relied on this axiom in his opinion in the case
of the Indigent Persons Act of California. Byrnes pointed out that
indigent non-residents, who had no opportunity to exert political
pressure on the California legislature, were the real victims of the
act. (314 U.S. at 174.)

When the legislature attacks the democratic process itself, let the Court fight for it. The first and still the best statement of this axiom is in a footnote that the then Justice, later Chief Justice, Harlan F. Stone put into the opinion he wrote for the Court in the *Carolene Products Company* case. (304 U.S. at 152-3.) You will admire the exceedingly restrained way Stone denied the need of any self-restraint, and meant, I am sure, no less than that the Court should fight. What Stone said, tucked into a footnote, was this:

"It is unnecessary to consider now whether legislation which restricts those political processes which can ordinarily be expected to bring about repeal of undesirable legislation is to be subjected to more exacting judicial scrutiny under the general prohibitions of the Fourteenth Amendment than are most other types of legislation." Stone then cites cases on restrictions upon the right to vote, on restraints upon the dissemination of information, on interferences with political organizations, and prohibition of peaceable assembly.

"Nor need we inquire whether similar considerations enter into the review of statutes directed at particular religious, or national, or racial minorities; whether prejudice against discrete and insular minorities may be a special condition, which tends seriously to curtail the operation of those political processes ordinarily to be relied upon to protect minorities, and which may call for a correspondingly more searching judicial inquiry."

This, I repeat, Stone tucked into a footnote. Let me put it in my own way: When the democratic process is working and the statute or whatnot is clearly the result of the working of that process, what shall the Court do then? He who fights and runs away, may live to fight another day. Or shall the Court start fighting on the beaches, go on fighting in the fields and in the streets, and fight on in the hills? Will there be another day? Heroics aside, that is the question.

Then there is Black's high opinion of the jury as a tribunal of justice. In the *Galloway* case (319 U.S. at 407), the trial court had taken the case away from the jury and directed a verdict for the defendant on the ground of insufficient evidence. The Court saw nothing wrong in that. Black dissented. He said, "The Court here re-examines testimony offered in a common law suit, weighs conflicting evidence, and holds that the litigant may never take this case to a jury. The founders of our government thought that trial of fact by juries rather than by judges was an essential bulwark of civil liberty. For this reason, among others, they adopted Article III, Section 2 of the Constitution, and the Sixth and Seventh Amendments. Today's decision marks a continuation of the gradual process of judicial erosion which in one hundred and fifty years has slowly worn away a major portion of the essential guarantee of the Seventh Amendment." And Black cited Jefferson: "I consider trial by jury as the only anchor ever yet imagined by man, by which a government can be held to the principles of its constitution."

Black has an aversion for the blue-ribbon jury. He regards it as unconstitutional, which is to say, not a jury at all. He and Douglas and Rutledge joined in Murphy's dissent in the New York blue-ribbon jury case, and their reason was this: "The vice lies in the very concept of 'blue-ribbon' panels—the systematic and intentional exclusion of all but the 'best' or the most learned or intelligent of the general jurors. Such panels are completely at war with the democratic theory of our jury system, a theory formulated out of the experience of generations. One is constitutionally entitled to be judged by a fair sampling of all one's neighbors who are qualified, not merely those with superior intelligence or learning." (*Moore* v. *N.Y.*, 333 U.S. 565; see also *Fay* v. *N.Y.*, 332 U.S. 261, for Jackson's opinion for the Court.)

This is pure Jefferson, who said, you will recall, "State a moral case to a ploughman and a professor. The former will decide it as well, and often better than the latter, because he has not been led astray by artificial rules." And I feel certain that Black believes as earnestly as

Jefferson did that justice is "instinct and innate, that the moral sense is as much a part of our constitution as that of feeling, seeing, or hearing; as a wise creator must have seen to be necessary in an animal destined to live in society."

Jefferson's irreverence for the past is well known, and it did not mellow with age. Listen to his views in 1816, a generation after the Revolution:

"Some men look at constitutions with sanctimonious reverence and deem them like the ark of the covenant, too sacred to be touched. They ascribe to the men of the preceding age a wisdom more than human and suppose what they did to be beyond amendment. I knew that age well; I belonged to it and labored with it. It deserved well of its country. It was very like the present, but without the experience of the present; and forty years of experience in government is worth a century of book-reading; and this they would say themselves, were they to rise from the dead. I am certainly not an advocate for frequent and untried changes in laws and constitutions. I think moderate imperfections had better be borne with; because, when once known, we accommodate ourselves to them and find practical means of correcting their ill effects.

"But I know also that laws and institutions must go hand in hand with the progress of the human mind. As that becomes more developed, more enlightened, as new discoveries are made, new truths disclosed, and manners and opinions change with the change of circumstances, institutions must advance also and keep pace with the times. We might as well require a man to wear still the coat which fitted him when a boy, as civilized society to remain ever under the regimen of their barbarous ancestors." (In a letter to Samuel Kercheval, July 12, 1816.)

Jefferson's metaphor of the boy's coat and the grown-up man goes to the heart of the matter. I wonder if he was here half remembering what one of the great Lord Chancellors had said. For Jefferson hit on the same notion that Francis Bacon dropped in the *Novum Organum*:

"As for antiquity, the opinion touching it which men entertain is quite a negligent one and scarcely consonant with the word itself. For the old age of the world is to be accounted the true antiquity, and this is the attribute of our own times, not of that earlier age of the world in which the ancients lived, and which, though in respect of us it was the elder, yet in respect of the world it was the younger. From our age, if it but knew its own strength and chose to essay and exert it, much more might fairly be expected than from the ancient times, in as much as it is a more advanced age of the world and stored and stocked with infinite experiments and observations."

One of our most respected and admired Chief Justices, Charles Evans Hughes, once dropped the remark in a lecture he was giving that "the Constitution is what the judges say it is." *Say* it *is,* not *said* it *was.* For, like it or not, the Constitution is an ambulatory document, which is to say, "We the people . . . do ordain and establish. . . ." We speak in the present tense.

What We keep repeating is the text of our Constitution. All that others have said about it are no more than footnotes or comments noted in the margin. *The Federalist* is no more than a preface. The commentaries, whether of Story or of Hand, have no more authority than the marginal notes of a previous owner. The opinions of the Supreme Court rise no higher than footnotes. Now the doctrine of *stare decisis,* which enjoins on the Court a reverence for its own precedents, directs its attention to the footnotes and away from the text. Every now and then—the back numbers of the *Journal of the American Bar Association* must be full of instances—you run across some jurist saying that an opinion of the Supreme Court becomes a part of the Constitution, alterable only by amendment. This is not, of course, *stare decisis.* Nor is it jural. It is ecclesiastical, an attempt to endow the Court with a papal infallibility.

Senator Black told the Senate, when he was debating his child-labor bill, "The Constitution is final, and no doctrine of *stare decisis* applies to opinions on constitutional interpretation." (Frank, p. 90.) And Justice Black has no more respect for the doctrine than the Senator had.

Let us see how close Black is on Jefferson's heels.

If Black thinks the text is clear, he is quite willing to ignore an established meaning, however firmly set in the precedents. In the first spring after his appointment, Black dissented alone in protest at a preposterous interpretation which the Court had taken for granted for fifty years.

I cannot convince you how preposterous it was, unless you read the Fourteenth Amendment, and then you will convince yourself. The Court held, without hearing argument and without giving any reasons, that corporations were "persons" who could not be deprived of their property without due process of law. This was in 1886, and I do not recall that it was questioned by any Justice until Black, in 1938, said he didn't believe it.

I am not questioning the wisdom of this ruling. On the contrary, when a court does something quite unjustified as a matter of law, a careful critic will cast about to see if there were not some better reason. Here, I take it, this must lie in the manifest wisdom, but not necessity, of giving corporations the rights and benefits that Congress meant for individuals, "persons" or "citizens," for the Amendment speaks of no one else. I am confirmed in this hypothesis by the fact that all subsequent Congresses, in their wisdom, have let the Court's ruling stand.

There has been a further development that is worth mentioning here, even if Black were not involved in it. Many corporations, as almost all of us are aware, have increased in power and in prestige, and they are attracting more of our loyalties than their fair share. William H. Whyte's Organization Man, at a point, may even become naturalized as a sort of corporate citizen. Corporations are even taking over governmental functions. Those having government contracts in fields of sensitive security are now expected, indeed required, to police their premises and everyone who works for them. Ralph S. Brown has recently finished a book about this intrusion of the corporation—the word is mine—into government. (*Loyalty and Security*, Yale University Press, 1958.)

Black is involved in all this through his opinion in the case of *Marsh* v. *Alabama* in 1945. (326 U.S. 501.) This was a fairly obvious case. A corporation owned and operated a company town. The Court, speaking through Black, held that the corporation was as amenable to the Fourteenth Amendment as a municipal corporation would be. Adolf Berle remarks that this brings the Court "within a biscuit toss" of applying the Amendment to corporations as well as to States. (*The 20th-Century Capitalist Revolution*, by Adolf A. Berle, Jr.; Harcourt, Brace, 1954.) The Court assimilated corporations to "persons." Black is assimilating them to "States." Thus, under a preposterous ruling that corporations as "persons" have the rights, it now looks, as the judicial mind progresses, as if they were to be subject also to the duties. A case of logical schizophrenia. (*Connecticut General Insurance Co.*, 303 U.S. 77; read *Wheeling Steel* v. *Glander*, 337 U.S. 562 for Jackson's and Douglas' comments.)

In the *South-Eastern Underwriters'* case, Black persuaded the Court to reverse a seventy-five-year-old precedent, which held that the business of insurance is not commerce. This is what the Court had held in 1869 and the Court had been repeating it ever since, until Black refused to believe it and persuaded the Court it wasn't so in 1944. Congress promptly passed an Act telling the States to continue to regulate their insurance companies. (322 U.S. 533.)

Black will gladly modernize an ancient phrase or term and bring it up to date. He got the Court to do just this in the *Lovett* case (328 U.S. 303), when the Dies Committee tried to run Robert Morss

Lovett out of the Government by cutting off his salary. If you will read Frankfurter's and Reed's dissent, you will see how thoroughly the Court was renovating the dusty phrase, a bill of attainder.

If Black finds that the text has left the issue open, he feels quite free to avail himself of his own understanding, as Kant put it. There is a recent case that carries this moral, the *Green* case, where the question was whether a criminal contempt could be tried by the judge or had to be tried by a jury. (356 U.S. 165; March 1958.)

Two of the eleven Communists who had been convicted of violating the Smith Act back in 1949 in the notorious trial over which Judge Medina had presided with such éclat had jumped their bail. They were fugitives from justice for four and a half years. Then they finally and voluntarily surrendered, and the judge held them in contempt of court, for their disobedience of the lawful order of the court, and sentenced them to three years more imprisonment, to commence after they served the five years for their violation of the Smith Act.

Judges have been trying contempts of court, criminal contempts as well as civil, without a jury from the very foundation of the Republic and earlier. Their power to do this had never been questioned, despite the constitutional requirement that "The Trial of all Crimes . . . shall be by Jury." Frankfurter listed two score of cases where the judge's power to punish contempts summarily had been accepted without question, and the names of fifty-three Justices of the Supreme Court who had sustained this power in the judge instead of a jury.

And yet no one seemed willing to distinguish sending a man to prison for contempt of court from any more usual crime. Holmes had said that contempt of court could not be distinguished from crimes and suggested that preferably they might be tried by the usual criminal procedure. (*Gompers* v. *U.S.* 233 U.S. at 610-611.) Professor Beale in a learned article had come to the conclusion that "though technically there is no constitutional objection to the trial of such a contempt without a jury . . . the same general considerations of justice which lead to a jury trial upon a charge of crime also lead to the conclusion that a jury trial in such a case, where it is practicable, is required." (*Harvard Law Review*, January 1908.) No one, that is, except Justice Black, Chief Justice Warren, and Justice Douglas. They dissented, and Black spoke for them. Here is the closing paragraph of his opinion:

"In the last analysis there is no justification in history, in necessity, or most important in the Constitution for trying those charged with violating a court's decree in a manner wholly different from those accused of disobeying any other mandate of the state. It is significant that neither the Court nor the Government makes any serious effort to justify such differentiation except that it has been sanctioned by prior decisions. . . . I can perceive nothing which places these decrees on any higher or different plane than the laws of Congress or the regulations of the Executive insofar as punishment for their violation is concerned. There is no valid reason why they should be singled out for an extraordinary and essentially arbitrary mode of enforcement. Unfortunately judges and lawyers have told each other the contrary so often that they have come to accept it as the gospel truth. In my judgment trial by the same procedures, constitutional and otherwise, which are extended to criminal defendants in all other instances is also wholly sufficient for the crime of contempt." (356 U.S. at 218; March 1958.)

Twenty years ago, after Black's first judicial year, I spoke of his "disrespect and distaste for judicial statesmanship." (*Atlantic Monthly* for May 1939.) What shall I say now, after his twenty judicial years?

I take it that the thing to do first is to turn to Black's bitter and at the same time his most intelligent critic. Justice Robert Jackson died in 1954, shortly before he was to deliver the Godkin lectures at Harvard.

They were published after his death. Jackson was going to say this, which was pretty plainly aimed at Black, among others:

"The question that the present times put into the minds of thoughtful people is to what extent Supreme Court interpretations of the Constitution will or can preserve the free government of which the Court is a part. A cult of libertarian judicial activists now assails the Court almost as bitterly for renouncing power as the earlier 'liberals' once did for assuming too much power. This cult appears to believe that the Court can find in a 4,000-word eighteenth-century document or its nineteenth-century Amendments, or can plausibly supply, some clear bulwark against all dangers and evils that today beset us internally. This assumes that the Court will be the dominant factor in shaping the constitutional practice of the future and can and will maintain, not only equality with the elective branches, but a large measure of supremacy and control over them. I may be biased against this attitude because it is so contrary to the doctrines of the critics of the Court, of whom I was one, at the time of the Roosevelt proposal to reorganize the judiciary. But it seems to me a doctrine wholly incompatible with faith in democracy, and insofar as it encourages a belief that the judges may be left to correct the result of public indifference to issues of liberty in choosing Presidents, Senators, and Representatives, it is a vicious teaching."

Just what is a "libertarian judicial activist"? Just what is an "activist"? Here again we run into the futility of a definition, but that's no reason not to try.

A member of Holmes' Society of Jobbists knows perfectly well what an activist is. He is someone who could never be elected to the Society. But if you are not a Jobbist, the term activist is hard to define. The best I can do is: someone who acts for what he believes the common good beyond the call of immediate duty. Someone, if you please, who acts over and above the call of duty and turns it into an opportunity to do good. Yet that's not it. Perhaps an activist is simply someone who treats his job as a means toward some nobler end. He's not just an artisan, he's an artist. A case is a cause. He's an Abou Ben Adhem.

Brandeis was an activist of the first water. Bickel, in his book, *The Unpublished Opinions of Mr. Justice Brandeis,* brings this out very clearly through Holmes, who was a Jobbist and the least likely to be mistaken for an activist:

"To Brandeis, the state was an instrument for the achievement of the highest good. In some areas this meant for him legislative freedom to experiment. But in others the state was morally bound to adhere to unchanging values, whose attainment was its ultimate end. It is to be doubted, on the other hand, whether for Holmes, with his persistent strain of positivism, the state, the territorial club, as he called it, was in this sense anything but a morally neutral fact; a prerequisite to the good life, yes, but quite helpless to create it. In a letter to Harold J. Laski, written late in 1930, Holmes alluded to this disparity between himself and Brandeis: 'I told him [Brandeis] long ago that he really was an advocate rather than a Judge. He is affected by his interest in a cause, and if he feels it he is not detached. . . .' But Holmes hastened to add that 'his interests are noble, and as you say his insights profound.' Much earlier, speaking of other men, Holmes had expressed in letters to Felix Frankfurter a thought which must have struck him as well in connection with Brandeis: 'It seems as if the gift of passionate enthusiasm were racial. It is a great one.' And: 'It seems as if an exquisite moral susceptibility were the gift of many Jews.' "

Of one thing, anyhow, we may be sure. It was an admirable activism that led Black to stand fast for our individual liberties and privacies against the manhandling they got from Senator McCarthy and his gangsters and against the loose-lipped fears that were his accessories. If Mr. Standfast be an activist, let him make the most of it.

This is no place—there is no room, no time—even to run through

Black's record. We must be content now with the compliment Senator James O. Eastland paid Black the other day when he publicized the "scores" of the Justices. For Black's name led all the rest. "Seventy-one times," Eastland said, "Justice Hugo Black voted to sustain the position advocated by the Communists, and not one vote or one case did he decide to the contrary. . . ." Douglas got sixty-six.

And so I say that Justice Black is a child of the eighteenth century and the spiritual heir of Thomas Jefferson. Are we not all of us his heirs? Are we not all children of the Enlightenment?

Last week I went to a small rally for Chester Bowles, who was running for Congress. He spoke of the Bandung Conference, which opened on April 18, 1955, and where twenty-nine nations were represented, over half the people of the world. The United States, out of an excess of caution, was not represented, but one of the speakers, Bowles said, recited verses from "The Midnight Ride of Paul Revere." This stirred me and I started wondering and inquiring. The next day I went to the annual dinner of the Massachusetts Historical Society. Arthur Schlesinger, Senior, spoke, in the very tongue, I may say, of Jefferson himself, and behold, he said that at Bandung, on the opening day of the Conference, the eighteenth of April, Sukarno, the President of Indonesia, seized on the anniversary to celebrate Lexington and Concord by reciting a stanza from "The Midnight Ride of Paul Revere"! Do we have to be told that we are children of our own revolution? Are we laggards in our brightest and boldest tradition?

Yes; and what is the best reply to the Communist Manifesto? Well, the Declaration of Independence is as good as any and better than none.

"The United States, child of the Enlightenment, favored adolescent of the nineteenth century, powerful but erratic youth of the first half of the twentieth"—this is Walt Rostow—"must now justify its manhood by acting from the present forward to see the values of the

Enlightenment—or their equivalents in non-Western cultures—survive and dominate in the twenty-first."

And now back to my question. Which do you choose? A judicial version of Natural Law for Today or our eighteenth-century Bill of Rights?

VII

You will understand that you do not have to choose. For we could insist upon Congress itself applying due process to the States. Or Congress could take it away from the Court and leave it where it used to be—in the hands of the States. This, I think, is where Black would like to see it, if I read the last paragraph of his Adamson dissent aright: ". . . a responsibility which the Constitution entrusts to the legislative representatives of the people." (332 U.S. at 92.) Or do you think Black is referring to Congress? Anyhow, Section Five of this Fourteenth Amendment says, "The Congress shall have power to enforce, by appropriate legislation, the provisions of this article." I don't see that this leaves any power to the Court beyond the question whether Congress acts "appropriately," except, of course, the power Congress allows the Court to exercise in its stead.

The power to enforce the provisions of the Amendment—that is, to require the States to respect "due process of law" and "the equal protection of the laws"—carries with it the power to say what those provisions mean. So you see where we are. Congress was here given the power, not only to restrain the States, but likewise the power to permit them to abridge our privileges, deprive us of our lives, liberties, and properties without observing due process of law, and power to deny us the equal protection of the laws.

This is a grave thought, and it is strange that the significance and the extent of this Section Five has not attracted more attention. So little consideration has been given it that we are justified in going back and seeing what the authors of the Amendment may have had in mind.

As we have seen, Black argued in his Adamson dissent that the true intent of the Fourteenth Amendment was simply to extend the Bill of Rights over the States. He attached a long historical memorandum to demonstrate this thesis. (332 U.S. at 92-123.) But Black is a better lawyer than historian, and I prefer the conclusion Charles Fairman came to. All he could find in the nature of intentions were what he calls "vague aspirations." (*Stanford Law Review* for December 1949.) Aspirations, those Congressmen who wrote and sponsored and passed the Amendment, back in 1866-1868, surely had. They were working in the fine flush of military triumph, immediately after the Civil War. They were celebrating—just what they did not know, but their mood must have had a sort of Fourth of July splendor. Fairman examined the record and, brooding over it, he says he was slowly brought to the conclusion that Cardozo's gloss in the *Palko* case (302 U.S. 319) on the due-process clause, what is implicit in the concept of ordered liberty, comes as close as he could get to catch these vague aspirations.

Roscoe Conkling was one of the authors, and in his argument before the Supreme Court in the *San Mateo* case (116 U.S. 138), where he persuaded the Court that corporations were people, i.e., "persons," Conkling's rhetoric brings us, I think, as close as we can get:

"Those who devised the Fourteenth Amendment wrought in grave sincerity. They may have builded better than they knew.

"They vitalized and energized a principle, as old and as everlasting as human rights. To some of them, the sunset of life may have given mystical lore.

"They builded, not for a day, but for all time; not for a few, or for a race, but for man. They planted in the Constitution a monumental truth, to stand four-square whatever wind might blow." (Charles Fairman's biography of Mr. Justice Miller, p. 188.)

I like so much the way C. Vann Woodward has put it that I am
going to borrow his words:

"The Union fought the Civil War on borrowed moral capital. With
their noble belief in their purpose and their extravagant faith in the
future, the radicals ran up a staggering war debt, a moral debt that
was soon found to be beyond the country's capacity to pay, given the
undeveloped state of its moral resources at the time. After making a
few token payments during Reconstruction, the United States defaulted
on the debt and unilaterally declared a moratorium that lasted more
than eight decades. The country was only nominally spared the for-
mality of bankruptcy by the injunctions of the Supreme Court that
cast doubt upon the validity of the debt. In the meantime, over the
years, interest on the debt accumulated. The debt was further
augmented by the shabby treatment of the forgotten creditors, our
own Negro citizens.

"Then, in the middle of the twentieth century, conscience finally
began to catch up with commitment. Very suddenly, relatively speaking, it became clear that the almost forgotten Civil War debt had to be
paid, paid in full, and without any more stalling than was necessary.
As in the case of the commitment to emancipation during the Civil
War, amoral forces and pressures such as the exigencies of foreign
propaganda, power politics, and military necessities exercised a powerful influence upon the recommitment to equality. But also as in the
case of emancipation, the voices of conscience, of national creed, and
of religious conviction played their part." (In *The American Scholar*
for Autumn 1958.)

Now there is only one satisfactory way to put aspirations into a
constitution, and that is by some hallowed phrase. Conkling and his
colleagues went about it in the right way. They saw that no definition
was possible. As Lord Samuel told the House of Lords in the course of
their debate over the abolition of capital punishment in 1956, "I think
it was Rousseau who said, 'Definitions would be very good things if

only we did not have to use words to make them with.' " (Hansard, p. 806; July 10, 1956.) So they chose some phrases hallowed by tradition and delegated their definition to Congress.

To Congress, mind you, not to the Court. In the course of a panel discussion in the New York University Law School a few years ago, John Frank asked Willard Hurst about the basic intention of this Amendment. Hurst said:

"Now it is pretty plain that the actual framers thought they were delegating the rule-making power to Congress, being confident as men so often are that they and like-minded people would always be the Congress. It is quite plain that the Supreme Court of the United States took the ball away from the Congress; but the fact remains that the basic intent was to set a broad and vague standard and to allow the standard to be defined as particular situations might call for definition. I don't think you can sensibly distinguish in that respect between the power of judges and the power of Congress even though Thaddeus Stevens meant primarily to give the power to Congress." (*Supreme Court & Supreme Law*, ed. by Edmond Cahn, Indiana University Press, 1954; p. 60.)

Stevens' Congress, the thirty-ninth, did undertake the task and enacted the Civil Rights Acts, but when the Radical Republicans lost power, Congress lost interest. Since then Congress has left the enforcement of the Fourteenth Amendment to the Court.

There was nothing wrong about this. Congress lost interest and we did not insist. We were satisfied to let the Court do it. To quote Fairman again:

"As our experience with the Fourteenth Amendment has unfolded it has been the Court to which the country has looked for authentic interpretation. Congress, which in the thinking of 1866 was to have so central a place, has come to play a minor role. It has seemed far more consistent with our polity that for the protection of fundamental rights the citizen look to the courts rather than be dependent upon the fluctuating views of the legislature. We say with pride that no man holds his rights by the leave of his fellows. So when the claim to desegregated treatment was presented in orderly litigation, the Court took not only the courageous but the normal course in deciding the issue itself." (*Harvard Law Review*, 1956, p. 85.)

No one can blame the Court, which has to decide the cases that come before it, for reading the Fourteenth Amendment with due regard for what it says, and then, with no guide from Congress of what it means, turning to tradition. And yet this was not an inescapable judicial duty, and when the Court finally came to decide whether the Amendment tolerated racial segregation in our schools the Court must have been under a good deal of temptation to pass the ball back to Congress.

Last March, Paul Freund told the London School of Economics what the Court had faced (*The Modern Law Review* for July 1958) :

"When the court was faced, finally, with the school cases, three lines of decision were open to it. It might have decided that the old separate-but-equal standard reflected the outermost limit of equal protection of the laws in the year 1954, that segregation enforced by law was consistent with the national understanding of the meaning of legal equality. Such a decision would surely have been found as repugnant as was, in different quarters, the decision actually reached. The court might, in the second place, have treated the issue as a 'political question,' to be determined by Congress under its specific power to legislate in order to carry out the provisions of the Fourteenth Amendment. This solution must have had a certain attraction for judges aware of the problems of enforcement of judicial decrees in this area. And yet to have resorted to this evasive solution would itself have created new law, since hitherto, for seventy-five years, Congress had left it to the court to develop the content of the equal-protection guarantee. To announce now that the responsibility rested in truth on Congress would have been something of an Alphonse-Gaston game, with no one going through the door."

"The court, instead, took the responsibility, and did so in measured stages, first announcing the principle of nonsegregation and later, after a delay for further argument of counsel, considering the form of the decree. The critical terms of the decree are, of course, 'deliberate speed'—a phrase taken from English Chancery practice and not, as some litterateurs believed, from the refrain in Francis Thompson's 'Hound of Heaven': 'deliberate speed, majestic instancy.' If poetic terms are insisted on, the court preferred Thompson's refrain (or the first part of it) to Keats': 'Thou foster-child of silence and slow time.' "

Yes, anything else would have been "an evasive solution," because it was quite plain to Alphonse that Congress, though it would bow as deeply as Gaston, was not going to go through that door. This was not the kind of Congress that the Thirty-ninth Congress had in mind when it proposed giving itself this power to enforce the Amendment. The kind of Congress the Thirty-ninth had in mind and the only kind that would assure the Negroes the equal protection of the laws was a Congress that had been elected in proper compliance with the other provision of the Fourteenth Amendment, with the representation of a State which denied a vote to any inhabitant over twenty-one proportionately reduced. It will take more insistence by us than it should to persuade Congress to relieve the Court of its responsibility and the necessity of doing its judicial duty. If the Court had run out on its line of precedents and asked the Congress to take this last hurdle because it seemed too high for short judicial legs, nothing would have been done, and the best the Court could say would be that the blame was shared.

However, what concerns us here is not the blame but what it does to the Court's constitutional role to be in so many important respects a stand-in for Congress, a *locum tenens,* a tenant at sufferance. Call it what you please, Congress has the last word. The Court has only the first. For any doctrine the Court declares can readily be reversed, modified, corrected, simply by an act of Congress—or allowed to stand. If the Court does anything wrong, Congress can make it right— barring, I should add, the decision in the case. As to the parties and their rights, of course the Court's decision stands.

Is a cause ever lost through unsuccess? The question would surely be raised by an account of our Supreme Court's attempt to bring due process of law into the criminal procedure of State courts, and were this the place for such an account, it might be given an answer.

"Of course," Frankfurter has said, "the Fourteenth Amendment is not to be applied so as to turn this Court into a tribunal for revision of criminal convictions in the State courts." (Dissenting in *Stein* v. *N.Y.*, 346 U.S. 156 at 199; this was the *Reader's Digest* murder in 1950.) Yet the Court has been trying to do just this for the last twenty years. For justice is like art; and art, as Wallace Stegner has remarked, is "all variables, all particulars." General propositions can no more do justice than they can decide concrete cases. Are not two sparrows sold for a farthing?

I think it was Black who started this crusade for a better justice in criminal cases with his opinion in the *Chambers* case. (309 U.S. 227; 1940.) There the Court unanimously reversed the convictions by a Florida court of four ignorant young colored tenant farmers for the murder of an elderly white man, because it seemed to the Court that their confessions had been improperly obtained. They had followed protracted questioning and cross-questioning by State officers and other white citizens in a fourth-floor jail room, where they were held without friends, advisers or counselors. These circumstances, the Court said, were "calculated to break the strongest nerves and the stoutest resistance." For five days the four boys steadily denied their guilt. Then they broke, and a jury convicted them. Black said:

"We are not impressed by the argument that law-enforcement methods such as those under review are necessary to uphold our laws.

The Constitution proscribes such lawless means irrespective of the end. And this argument flouts the basic principle that all people must stand on an equality before the bar of justice in every American court. Today, as in ages past, we are not without tragic proof that the exalted power of some governments to punish manufactured crime dictatorially is the handmaid of tyranny. Under our constitutional system, courts stand against any winds that blow as havens of refuge for those who might otherwise suffer because they are helpless, weak, outnumbered, or because they are nonconforming victims of prejudice and public excitement. Due process of law, preserved for all by our Constitution, commands that no such practice as that disclosed by this record shall send any accused to his death. No higher duty, no more solemn responsibility, rests upon this Court than that of translating into living law and maintaining this constitutional shield deliberately planned and inscribed for the benefit of every human being subject to our Constitution—of whatever race, creed or persuasion."

From year to year the Court has been taking up a few such cases, and it insists on making "our own examination of the record to determine whether the claim is meritorious. The performance of this duty cannot be foreclosed by the finding of a court, or the verdict of a jury, or both." I quote from a good recent example, the case of *Payne* v. *Arkansas* (356 U.S. 560), in the spring of 1958, of a coerced confession from a nineteen-year-old Negro convicted of murder.

Can such a cause be lost? Can such passion for justice ever be satisfied? The mills of God do indeed grind as minutely as they are said to do, because God has all the time in the world and a passion for detail. Is not John Raeburn Green right when he says, "Each right should be considered on its own merits, not each trial on its own merits. The Bill of Rights safeguards the rights of the accused, not simply to aid a particular individual in a particular trial, but in order to protect a free society against the excesses of power and to provide an efficient administration of justice. The rights ought then to be examined, one at a time, as they come to the Court, with regard to their inclusion either in due process or in liberty." (In *Essays in Constitutional Law*, ed. by R. G. McCloskey, Knopf, 1957; p. 427.)

John P. Frank, on the other hand, blames the Court, not the undertaking. In his recent book, *Marble Palace, The Supreme Court in American Life* (Knopf, 1958; p. 220), Frank sees the Court shilly-shallying:

"Where state criminal justice is concerned, the Court has balanced one foot forward with one foot back. The grosser types of forced confessions, for example, have been repudiated by the Court, as when in a Mississippi case Negro defendants were taken by the police into the forest, tied to trees, and beaten to a pulp; or the cases in which defendants have been detained incommunicado for many days subject to prolonged interrogation under bright lights, without friends or counsel, without food, and usually without sleep. Yet these abuses are the inevitable concomitance of any secret detention and interrogation, for the rubber hose is always the lazy man's substitute for first-class detection; it is probably not accidental that the F.B.I. is almost never charged with these abuses, perhaps because the talents of its members make rubber hoses unnecessary. The Court has largely failed to afford a clear-cut constitutional rule for the states to follow—e.g., that persons seized by state police shall not be held and questioned without the filing of formal charges.

"The tendency of the Court when reviewing state criminal cases is to make distinctions so fine that the general run of state trial courts can be expected to pay little attention to them. . . .

"There has been no serious over-all appraisal of the practical consequences of Supreme Court supervision of state criminal justice in the last twenty-five years. A prodigious job of fact-gathering and analysis would be necessary to form any thoughtful opinion as to whether or not the Court has made a substantial contribution in this field. There is grave room for doubt. The Court can handle only an infinitesimal number of all the cases in the country, and where it fails to draw sharp, clean lines, it may as well, for national-leadership purposes, throw in the sponge. There is no area on the civil-rights horizon in which the lines of Court policy are more fuzzy and unclear than in this one."

So far as I am concerned, both are right. Green sizes up the magnitude of the undertaking, which is surely magnificent and which, I may add, he calls "natural law at its worst." Frank appreciates that great causes call for great efforts. But my concern is with my thesis here, and so all I say is this.

Here's a problem that Congress can solve if it wants to. Congress could, quite simply, enact the American Law Institute's Model Code of Criminal Procedure for all State courts, as well as for the Federal courts, as embodying Congress' notion of what due process is in criminal law. Section Five of this, the Fourteenth Amendment, gives Congress power to do this. Or, of course, Congress may prefer to watch the Court struggle.

It will not surprise you that the State judges resent what they regard as intrusions. You will, I think, agree with what Jackson said in one of his Godkin lectures—those he would have given at Harvard in 1955, had he not died. He said:

"Today, however, we have a different application of the Fourteenth Amendment. Today it is being used not to restrain State Legislatures but to set aside the acts of state courts, particularly in criminal matters. This practice has proceeded to a point where the Federal courts are in acute controversy with the State courts, and the assembled Chief Justices of the State courts have adopted severe resolutions condemning the Federal intervention.

"I must say that I am rather in sympathy with the Chief Justices of the State courts on this subject. I believe we are unjustifiably invading the rights of the States by expanding the constitutional concept of due process to include the idea that the error of a trial court deprives it of

'jurisdiction' by including in the concept by interpretation all other
constitutional provisions not literally incorporated in the Fourteenth
Amendment, and, in the alternative, by incorporating into it all of
our ideas of decency, even to the point of making a constitutional issue of rulings upon evidence." (Harvard University Press; p. 69.)

Three years later, when the Chief Justices of the States met in their
annual conference in August 1958 at Pasadena, they went further.
They expressed concern about the whole field of Federal-State relations. By a vote of 36 to 8, they passed resolutions approving a report of one of their committees. One ran as follows:

"Resolved:

"That this conference hereby respectfully urges that the Supreme
Court of the United States, in exercising the great powers confided to
it for the determination of questions as to the allocation and extent of
national and State powers, respectively, and as to the validity under
the Federal Constitution of the exercise of powers reserved to the
States, exercise one of the greatest of all judicial powers—the power
of judicial self-restraint—by recognizing and giving effect to the difference between that which, on the one hand, the Constitution may
prescribe or permit, and that which, on the other, a majority of the
Supreme Court, as from time to time constituted, may deem desirable
or undesirable, to the end that our system of federalism may continue
to function with and through the preservation of local self-government."

Not Congress, the Court. The Chief Justices did not look to Congress for relief or remedy. They asked only for a little self-restraint on
the part of the Court, as if the final responsibility for "the allocation
and extent of national and State powers respectively" lay on the knees
of the Court, and not in Congress. You and I know better. I wonder if
these Chief Justices may not have had compunctions about going over
the Court's head and appealing to Congress to take the matter out of
the Court's hands.

And yet every instance, every decision that the report cites to show that the Court has intruded on State power and State court jurisdiction could quite easily have been restrained or corrected by Congress, and they crisscross and cover nearly the whole field of Federal-State relations.

We have no need even to run through these decisions here. The report mentioned or discussed some twenty of them, all recent. Almost all of them were under the due-process clause of the Fourteenth Amendment, and I have already said enough about that. Four of them concerned interstate commerce, and here the report conceded that the state in which the law had been left was "in part undoubtedly due to the failure of Congress to make its wishes entirely clear." Another was a case where the Court had affirmed the decision of the Supreme Court of Pennsylvania that Congress had pre-empted the field of sedition and security. I may add that the Chief Justice of Pennsylvania was one of the eight who dissented from the report.

But the point I want to make is simply that every one of the twenty-odd decisions of the Court of greatest interest and most concern to the States was under the eye and subject to the correction of Congress. If the Court was acting as if it were a third chamber, a super legislature, the Congress could at any time have acted as a super super one.

What I have been saying about the Court's exercise of legislative power under the Fourteenth Amendment is equally true of very nearly all the Constitution's restrictions on the States. To a greater extent than our respect for the Court and our devotion to the doctrine of judicial supremacy permit us to appreciate, it is Congress, not the Court, which has the last word on these restrictions on the States.

"I do not think," Holmes said, in the plenitude of his wisdom, "the United States would come to an end if we lost our power to declare an Act of Congress void. I do think the Union would be imperiled if we could not make that declaration as to the laws of the several States."

Holmes then referred to the Commerce Clause, which gives Congress the power to regulate commerce between the States. If there is another provision in the Constitution that gives the States more concern and the Court more work than the Fourteenth Amendment, it is the Commerce Clause. For, though Congress has not neglected this power, the field has been too vast for Congress to cover except as occasion offered and demand pressed. So the field was open to intrusion and trespass by the States, each in pursuit of its own local interests. The Court stepped in at an early date; and Hand agrees "that it was not altogether irrational for Marshall and the Court to ask themselves whether, if 'commerce among the States' were left open to State regulation, there might not arise such a tangle of conflicts as would tend not only to strain the whole national fabric but to impede the eventual assertion of the power of Congress because of the vested interests that might have grown up."

What the Court did was hold unconstitutional any attempt by a State to regulate or to tax commerce with another State on a matter which, in the opinion of the Court, admitted only of one uniform plan or system. There the Court held that the power of Congress was exclusive, even when Congress was silent. You cannot very well call this a judicial question. It is not. Whether a subject admits of only one uniform plan of regulation involves a consideration on practical grounds of what is expedient, what is possible, what is desirable. It is legislation. (J. B. Thayer, in his *Cases on Constitutional Law,* II, 2190-1.)

The point is that Congress may act at any time and take over as much or as little as it chooses. Until then the Court is acting as a sort of game warden keeping the States from poaching or squatting or vesting their provincial interests. I scarcely need say how valuable the Court's services have been. Listen to Jackson:

"The extent to which State legislation may be allowed to affect the conduct of interstate business in the absence of Congressional action on the subject has long been a vexatious problem. Recently the tendency has been to abandon the earlier limitations and to sustain more freely such State laws on the ground that Congress has power to supersede them with regulation of its own. It is a tempting escape from a difficult question to pass to Congress the responsibility for continued existence of local restraints and obstructions to national commerce. But these restraints are individually too petty, too diversified, and too local to get the attention of a Congress hard pressed with more urgent matters. The practical result is that in default of action by us they will go on suffocating and retarding and Balkanizing American commerce, trade, and industry." (*Duckworth* v. *Arkansas,* 314 U.S. 390 at 400.)

If the Court is to tell the States when to stand back and do nothing that may impede what Congress has not yet done, but may do, about interstate commerce, the Court may likewise tell the States to keep their hands off what Congress is doing and tell the States this even when Congress has not itself said so in so many words. Here too the Court is legislating, for it is doing only what Congress did not do but could very well have done—that is, say whether it wanted its legislation to supersede State action and be free not only of any interference but also of inconvenient co-operation.

This is of small importance compared to the Commerce Clause and the Fourteenth Amendment, but the Court's decision a couple of years ago in the *Nelson* case (350 U.S. 497) wasted enough of Congress' time during the summer of 1958 to make it seem important. The Court sustained a decision of the Supreme Court of Pennsylvania that its Sedition Act had been superseded by the Federal so-called Smith Act of 1940, which, the Pennsylvania court held, had preempted the field of sedition. Steve Nelson, a Communist leader, had been convicted under the Pennsylvania statute. This let him off. A bill to correct the Court's decision passed the House by a large majority and was defeated in the Senate, after three days of debate, by a vote of 41 to 40.

The Court was plainly right and the forty Senators stupidly wrong, for the prosecution of Communists can be more effectively conducted under the Smith Act alone than amid the conflicts and confusions of forty-odd different State statutes. But there is no doubt whatsoever that Congress may, with or without wisdom, correct the Court in such a case.

The truth is, the restrictions the Constitution placed upon the States and on which the Supreme Court has the last word are unimportant compared with the restrictions that the Congress may place upon them and on which the Court speaks subject to Congressional correction. They are all in Section Ten of Article I. You will see how eagerly the most rabid States-righter would settle for them. Here they all are:

"No State shall enter into any Treaty, Alliance, or Confederation; grant Letters of Marque and Reprisal; coin Money; emit Bills of Credit; make any Thing but gold and silver coin a Tender in Payment of Debts; pass any Bill of Attainder, ex post facto Law, or Law impairing the Obligation of Contracts, or grant any Title of Nobility."

In every other respect, any doctrine, any rule that the Court makes restricting the powers of the States, is done under the eye of Congress and is subject to reversal or revision by act of Congress—or, to be sure, Congress can acquiesce and let it stand.

You will note that I am laying to one side what Lord Bryce called the "joint in the Court's armor." This is the power Congress has to take away the Court's appellate jurisdiction, which gives the Court all but a handful of the cases that come before it, and on which the Court's power and prestige rest. For, as you know, the Constitution subjects the Court's appellate jurisdiction, from State courts as well as Federal courts, to "such Exceptions and under such Regulations as the Congress shall make." Only once, in 1869, has Congress used this power to retaliate and prevent the Court from doing what the Congress did not want done. It is a recurrent threat, as the Butler and Jenner bills last summer showed, but not, I think, more. Besides, there is some question whether this power is as complete as Congress thinks it is. Henry M. Hart, Jr., has raised doubts. (66 *Harvard Law Review* 1362; 1953.) As a matter of fact, then, what Bryce called a joint is no more than a chink. We need the Court too much to maim or mutilate it out of resentment or spite. We believe, as Hand does, that its authority to speak the final word on whether Congress and the President have overstepped their powers is a "necessity in such a system as ours," "necessary to prevent the failure of the undertaking."

At the same time, Congress is coming more and more to distinguish between matters on which the Court acts with a final authority and its exercise of these legislative powers I have been describing, on which Congress, not the Court, has the final word. Here Congress is becoming aware of its powers.

Judge Charles E. Wyzanski, who sometimes seems to know almost as much about what's to come as he does about the present and the past, spoke in June 1958, at Harvard, and said:

"There are some of us who suppose that the Butler and Jenner bills are isolated phenomena, that they represent irritation at particular decisions of the Supreme Court, or that they are a reflex of the segregation controversy. But I suggest to you that though extreme in form, the Butler and Jenner bills represent a relationship which has been growing up between the Legislature and the Supreme Court, between Congress and the Court, and that no longer do we accept as ultimate authority the nine votes of the Supreme Court of the United States; more and more we are engaged in a constant revision by the Legislature of the Court, just as the Court revises the administrative agencies; and the degree of interdependence is constantly increasing. I do not deplore this, but I point out that one of the effects is that the central core of tradition which to a large extent binds judges is no longer fully operative in this situation, that to a much greater extent the concourse of interests, the conscious awareness of pressures, dominates the situation with a smaller role for a central core of value."

Here, in these fields, as we have seen, the Court is acting by leave of the Congress, legislating in lieu of Congress, and so quite properly subject to Congressional correction. There is, therefore, nothing derogatory of the Court's dignity when Congress does correct it, and no one can properly blame the Court when Congress acquiesces.

As you perceive, I have been trying to defend the Court against Hand's charge that it was guilty of a *coup de main,* and I think I have succeeded. Hand said that he had never been able to understand on what basis the Court's role as a third legislative chamber rested, or could rest, except as a *coup de main.* Here it is. The Court is absolved of its seizure of legislative power for the same reason Jonathan Wild so narrowly escaped being guilty of rape: ". . . he in a few minutes ravished this fair creature, or at least would have ravished her, if she had not, by a timely compliance, prevented him."

VIII

I COME to a nobler as well as a chaster theme. I want to see whether the Court's retention of the role of a third legislative chamber is justified. I may put it this way: Is the Court, should the Court be, the Prophet of our natural law, this Natural Law for Today? I think we agree that the stone that the builder refused fits, but have we put it in the right building? I am not at all sure.

We should begin with an excursion beyond law into society at large, for this modern version of natural law is a component of law only because it pervades society, giving our life in common its texture and its toughness. We should by rights spend as much time and attention examining this natural law outside of the law as we spend on it inside the law. But there's no time for such an excursion. The best I can do is turn you over to Walter Lippmann and press into your hand for a guidebook his recent book, *The Public Philosophy*. Then we should get at least a glimpse of the country that lies beyond, where there is no law.

Here are four or five paragraphs from Lippmann. What he calls "public philosophy" I have been calling natural law.

"We come, then, to a crucial question. If the discussion of public philosophy has been, so to speak, tabled in the liberal democracies, can we assume that, though it is not being discussed, there is a public philosophy? Is there a body of positive principles and precepts which a good citizen cannot deny or ignore? I am writing this book in the conviction that there is. It is a conviction which I have acquired gradually, not so much from a theoretical education, but rather from the practical experience of seeing how hard it is for our generation to make democracy work. I believe there is a public philosophy. Indeed there is such a thing as the public philosophy of civility. It does not have to be discovered or invented. It is known. But it does have to be revived and renewed.

"The public philosophy is known as *natural law,* a name which, alas, causes great semantic confusion. This philosophy is the premise of the institutions of the Western society, and they are, I believe, unworkable in communities that do not adhere to it. Except on the premises of this philosophy, it is impossible to reach intelligible and workable conceptions of popular election, majority rule, representative assemblies, free speech, loyalty, property, corporations, and voluntary associations. The founders of these institutions, which the recently enfranchised democracies have inherited, were all of them adherents of some one of the various schools of natural law.

"In our time the institutions built upon the foundations of the public philosophy still stand. But they are used by a public who are not being taught, and no longer adhere to, the philosophy. Increasingly, the people are alienated from the inner principles of their institutions. The question is whether and how this alienation can be overcome, and the rupture of the traditions of civility repaired.

"Needless to say I am not about to argue that the rupture can be repaired by a neo-classical or neo-medieval restoration, or by some kind of romantic return to feudalism, folk-dancing, and handicrafts. We cannot rub out the modern age, we cannot roll back the history that has made us what we are. We cannot start again as if there had been no advance of science, no spread of rationalism and secularism, no industrial revolution, no dissolution of the old habitual order of things, no sudden increase in the population. The poignant question is whether and, if so, how modern men could make vital contact with the lost traditions of civility.

"The appearance of things is quite obviously unpromising. There is radical novelty in our modern ways of life. The climate of feeling and the style of thought have changed radically. Modern men will first need to be convinced that the traditions of civility were not abandoned because they became antiquated. This is one of the roots of their unbelief and there is no denying its depth. Since the public philosophy preceded the advance of modern science and the industrial revolution, how can it be expected to provide a positive doctrine which is directly and practically relevant to the age we live in?"

This, as you see, is just what I have been trying to do, more optimistically than Lippmann and perhaps with too much assurance.

In the *Yale Review* for June 1955, Archibald MacLeish challenged Lippmann in the name of "the boundless liberty of the individual human spirit."

"What is novel in Mr. Lippmann's account is the fact that it is one of the most habituated of democratic journalists who advances the contention that true freedom in America ended with the end of the recognition of Natural Law in the late eighteenth century, and that the whole conception of the boundless liberty of the individual human spirit to which our own Republic has since been committed is a wrong steer, a tragic error.

"It is one thing for an American, thoroughly familiar with the American situation, to assert that our position is dangerous and our society far from perfect. Most of us are aware that mass vulgarity afflicts our culture and mass hysteria our politics and that the government of the Republic is increasingly difficult. It is another thing altogether for such a commentator to assert that the ideas which have made a nation of us—the ideas which have shaped our development since the beginning of the nineteenth century—are pernicious ideas which should now be renounced: that the modern democratic belief in the greatest possible individual freedom itself is false doctrine. . . .

"One may or may not like the characteristic art of our epoch. One may regard its characteristic quality as a kind of fad—a passing by-product of the investigations of Freud and Jung. There is perhaps some basis for such an opinion. Freud and Jung and their colleagues have powerfully influenced all our contemporaries, and the manner of some modern art is undoubtedly mannerism. But the fact remains that modern art did not begin with the modern psychologists: Baudelaire had written the *Fleurs du Mal* and Rimbaud had written the *Illuminations* before modern psychology was born. And the further fact is that the direction of modern art is not a direction which the modern artists alone have devised. It is not an invented or a perverse or a wayward direction. It is the direction of all conscious life, for the realization of consciousness is the end which all such life must seek. What modern art means is merely that mankind has crossed over, not secretly and surreptitiously but openly now, into that inward country. We no longer assume the superior reality of the public world of objective reason. We assume instead the deeper reality of the world within—which is to say, the world which each human individual uniquely is. . . ."

Lippmann's reply, in the same number of the *Yale Review*, makes it clear that this is what we were looking for, a glimpse beyond and into the country that lies on the farther side of all law. We too often take it for granted, even in this semi-civilized era, that nowhere is there no law.

"The crucial question, as between Mr. MacLeish's essay and my book, is why he and I, each believing he is on the side of the angels, appear to differ so much on what is the idea of freedom as it has been understood in this republic. The concluding chapters of my book are concerned with the very issue on which we differ, and with what I have learned to believe is the way that the wisest men in the Western tradition have dealt with that issue.

"Before we can deal with that issue, we must define it, and in his essay Mr. MacLeish has not, I submit, made the indispensable preliminary effort of clarification. He has two profoundly different but unseparated and undistinguished ideas of freedom. In some passages he holds that since the eighteenth century the American conception of freedom has been that 'of the boundless liberty of the *individual human spirit*.' But in at least one passage he speaks of 'the modern democratic belief in the greatest *possible* individual freedom.'

"Mr. MacLeish writes as if he thought he was saying the same thing in different words. But in my view there are here—as there are in the nature of things—not one idea of freedom but two ideas. In the one liberty is 'boundless.' In the other it is only as great as 'possible'; it has bounds though they are to be made as wide as is possible.

"It is with the relation of these two ideas of freedom that much of my book is concerned. They can be related, and accommodated the one with the other in human affairs, only if we begin 'by recognizing,' as I put it in my book, 'the difference between the realm of existence, where objects are materialized to our senses, and the realm of essence, where they are present to the mind.' "

"With Mr. MacLeish I believe in the 'boundless liberty of the *individual human spirit*.' But I do not believe, and neither can he, that boundless liberty is 'possible' in the public actions of everyone. The realm where liberty is 'boundless' is in the realm of essence, in what Mr. MacLeish in his peroration so aptly calls 'the inward country.' But in the outward country, in the public country of the diverse inhabitants of our plural society, freedom cannot be *boundless*. It can be only as great as is *possible*.

"In the outward and public country there are bounds upon the freedom of individuals, and it is the business of political philosophy to discern where in the conditions of the historical period the bounds have to be, and where they do not have to be—in order that there shall be as much freedom as is possible for all individuals. If free men do not keep their public actions within the bounds, they will make free government unworkable, and in the ensuing disasters and disorders freedom will be lost. The Greeks were the first to realize this. And this republic was founded by men who were deeply and earnestly aware of this truth.

"The mortal disease of free societies is to confuse the two realms, and to practice in the public world not a constitutional liberty but that boundless liberty which belongs to the inward country of the individual human spirit. That inward country may be the consciousness of genius and of a benefactor of mankind. It may be also the inward country of a Hitler or a McCarthy."

MacLeish's "inward country" is a land without law. It lies beyond law. For "a man can take law from others, but he finds it naturally impossible to give law to himself." Thoreau must surely have had this land in mind when he remarked, appropriately enough in his essay on the "Duty of Civil Disobedience," "It is not so important that many should be as good as you, as that there be some absolute goodness somewhere; for that will leaven the whole lump." Or enough absolute evil to poison it.

But we are concerned with the domain of law, where the sovereignty is shared by the positive law and natural law, Lippmann's "public philosophy." Side by side, in equal dignity, they walk behind the great mace, the staff of their authority, which is at once a stick to beat us and a wand to conjure with. As MacLeish makes clear, the law we give ourselves is no law. The positive law which the state gives us is half law. The other, and indispensable, half is our natural law, and this we get from each other. It is taught, not told. We learn it. We have to learn it, the farm boy notwithstanding, because the fact is that only by learning it are we enacting it.

I know as well as you or Thoreau how true it is that "more than any" the Poet "stands in the midst of Nature, yet more than any he can stand aloof from her." But I know too that this is as true of judges as it is of poets. After all, what else is it that makes natural law so different from the positive law, if it is not the fact that our natural law is in the midst of us?

IX

I S NOT THIS about where we came in? Though this new natural law I have been insisting on is not so innate as the farmer's boy took for granted, yet, if the way we learn it is from each other, teaching it to each other, why do we want lawyers and judges to tell it to us? Do they know any more about it than we know already?

Can't we do better than have our deepest feelings of right and wrong, our nicest distinctions between what's good and what's bad, our taste for the proper and our distaste at improprieties, yes, and what is neighborly or friendly and what is neither, our whole scale of values and our appraisal of sacrifices, our inarticulate premises and undistributed middles—can't we do better than go to lawyers for them, as if they were no different from the rest of the law? George Savile, that sagacious Marquess of Halifax, remarked, "If the laws could speak for themselves, they would complain of the lawyers in the first place."

This natural component in the law is not lawyers' law. To a lawyer, it is not really law at all but fact. Only the positive component is truly law to a lawyer, as any well-trained lawyer will agree, if I but remind him of a passage by Joseph Beale. It is in his treatise on the Conflict of Laws (Section 118):

"In the last analysis the law under which we live is as much a fact of our lives as the officers who administer that law. Any differentiation, therefore, between law and fact cannot rest upon any real or logical difference between them. The body of principles which we call law

86

does not differ in kind from the body of principles which we call ethics. It is only to the lawyer that law and fact offer themselves as opposing categories, and this distinction in the lawyer's mind reduces itself to a distinction between what he ought to know as a lawyer and the facts of which a lawyer has no peculiar knowledge. To the learned lawyer, and especially to the really learned judge, law is a part of himself, a part of his actual thought and existence. The thought of my nearest friend is to me a fact, while my own is something more than that; it is my experience and my life. In this way his law presents itself to one who is really learned in it.

"Such a man solving a legal problem presented to him does not say, Such and such a solution seems reasonable or reaches a practical result; he says, It is law. To a learned judge, argument of counsel is not instruction. It does not purport or attempt to tell him what he does not already know. Argument recalls, stimulates, or corrects in a judge his own line of thought. A sound judge in deciding a case does not consciously exercise his will to reach a new interpretation or a new development of law. He merely follows out his own line of thought as a lawyer and registers the conclusion to which he is led as a lawyer by this line of thought. Law, to a lawyer, is a part of his own mind; and it is only thus that it differs from fact."

Lawyers know no more about this natural law than we do, now that they admit that it is no longer a matter of revelation, either divine or rational, but, so far as they are concerned, matter of fact. You see we have come across another of our field marks.

An alien can be deported if he has committed "a crime involving moral turpitude." DeGeorge was a bootlegger and he had not paid the revenue taxes. The Court said this was defrauding the Government and "the decided cases make it plain that crimes in which fraud was an ingredient have always been regarded as involving moral turpitude."

Black, Frankfurter, and Jackson dissented. To them, "moral turpitude" was not "an intelligible definition of deportable conduct." (*Jordan* v. *DeGeorge*, 341 U.S. 223 at 245.)

It was argued on behalf of the Government that the nature of the crime "must be measured against the moral standards that prevail in contemporary society to determine whether the violations are generally considered essentially immoral." (Page 237.)

Jackson, who spoke for the three dissenters, asked, "Can we accept 'the moral standards that prevail in contemporary society' as a sufficiently definite standard for the purposes of the Act? This is a large country and acts that are regarded as criminal in some states are lawful in others. We suspect that moral standards which prevail as to possession or sale of liquor that has evaded tax may not be uniform in all parts of the country, nor in all levels of 'contemporary society.' How should we ascertain the moral sentiments of masses of persons on any better basis than a guess?"

Jackson went on to discuss the morals of it, and I can't help following him.

"The Court concludes that fraud is a 'contaminating component in any crime' and imports 'moral turpitude.' The fraud involved here is nonpayment of a tax. The alien possessed and apparently trafficked in liquor without paying the Government its tax. That, of course, is a fraud on the revenues. But those who deplore the traffic regard it as much an exhibition of moral turpitude for the Government to share its revenues as for respondents to withhold them. Those others who enjoy the traffic are not notable for scruples as to whether liquor has a law-abiding pedigree. So far as this offense is concerned with whisky, it is not particularly un-American, and we see no reason to strain to make the penalty for the same act so much more severe in the case of an alien 'bootlegger' than it is in the case of a native 'moonshiner.' I have never discovered that disregard of the nation's liquor taxes excluded a citizen from our best society, and I see no reason why it should banish an alien from our worst. . . .

"We should not forget that criminality is one thing—a matter of law—and that morality, ethics, and religious teachings are another. Their relations have puzzled the best of men. Assassination, for example, whose criminality no one doubts, has been the subject of serious debate as to its morality. This does not make crime less criminal, but it shows on what treacherous grounds we tread when we undertake to translate ethical concepts into legal ones, case by case. We usually end up by condemning all that we personally disapprove and for no better reason than that we disapprove it. In fact, what better reason is there? Uniformity and equal protection of the law can come only from a statutory definition of fairly stable and confined bounds."

Here are three highly intelligent lawyers saying that they find a phrase unintelligible which you and I have no difficulty at all in understanding. You will have your notion, I will have mine, and Jackson and Black and Frankfurter, each of them, will have theirs. Each of us, as Jackson remarks, will end up condemning what he disapproves for no better reason than that he disapproves. And, as he says, "what better reason is there?" And this, please observe, is why the law, as wise as any lawyer, does not ask a jury to give any reason for its verdict.

What do you think of a man who quite deliberately married his niece and had four children from her? Is he "a person of good moral character"? Would you naturalize him? Let us see what Hand concluded.

"Francioso was born in Italy in 1905, immigrated into the United States in 1923, and declared his intention of becoming a citizen in 1924. His wife was born in Italy in 1906, immigrated in 1911, and has remained here since then. They were married in Connecticut on February 13, 1925, and have four children, born in 1926, 1927, 1930, and 1933. Francioso was the uncle of his wife and knew when he

married her that the marriage was unlawful in Connecticut and that
the magistrate would not have married them, had they not suppressed
their relationship. They have always lived together in apparent concord, and at some time which the record leaves indefinite, a priest of
the Catholic Church—of which both spouses are communicants—
'solemnized' the marriage with the consent of his bishop. . . .

"In 1938 Francioso's children were five, eight, eleven, and twelve
years old, and his wife was 31; he was morally and legally responsible
for their nurture and at least morally responsible for hers. Cato himself would not have demanded that he should turn all five adrift. True,
he might have left the home and supported them out of his earnings;
but to do so would deprive his children of the protection, guidance, and
solace of a father. We can think of no course open to him which would
not have been regarded as more immoral than that which he followed,
unless it be that he should live at home, but as a celibate. There may
be purists who would insist that this alone was consistent with 'good
moral conduct'; but we do not believe that the conscience of the
ordinary man demands that degree of ascesis; and we have for warrant the fact that the Church—least of all complaisant with sexual
lapses—saw fit to sanction the continuance of this union." (*United
States* v. *Francioso*, 164 Fed. Rep. 2d 163-4; L. Hand, C.J.)

Do not be misled into thinking that Hand was relying on the
Church. Soon after this case of incest, another naturalization raised
the question whether a murderer could be of "a good moral character."
It was a case of euthanasia, and Hand said, "Left at large as we
are, without means of verifying our conclusion, and without authority
to substitute our individual beliefs, the outcome must needs be tentative; and not much is gained by discussion. We can say no more than
that, quite independently of what may be the current moral feeling
as to legally administered euthanasia, we feel reasonably secure in
holding that only a minority of virtuous persons would deem the
practice morally justifiable, while it remains in private hands, even

when the provocation is as overwhelming as it was in this instance."
So naturalization was denied, without prejudice, however, to a new
petition after the five years of "good moral character" after the
murder had elapsed. Judge Jerome Frank dissented, wanting to consult "our ethical leaders." He remarked:

"My colleagues, although their sources of information concerning
the pertinent mores are not shown to be superior to those of the
district judge, reject his finding. And they do so, too, while conceding
that their own conclusion is uncertain and (as they put it) 'tentative.'
I incline to think that the correct statutory test (the test Congress
intended) is the attitude of our ethical leaders. That attitude would not
be too difficult to learn; indeed, my colleagues indicate that they think
such leaders would agree with the district judge. But the precedents
in this circuit constrain us to be guided by contemporary public
opinion about which, cloistered as judges are, we have but vague
notions. One recalls Gibbon's remark that usually a person who talks
of 'the opinion of the world at large' is really referring to 'the few
people with whom I happened to converse.' " (Repouille v. United
States, 165 Fed. Rep. 2d, 154.)

No, the judges are on their own. They have no one to consult; nor
should they have anyone. A poll would be preposterous, and if the
First Amendment keeps governmental hands off our churches, surely
it keeps the clergy away from our bench. Later, in a similar case,
Hand would put it this way. "Even though we could take a poll, it
would not be enough merely to count heads, without any appraisal of
the voters. A majority of the votes of those in prisons and brothels,
for instance, ought scarcely to outweigh the votes of accredited church-
goers. Nor can we see any reason to suppose that the opinion of
clergymen would be a more reliable estimate than our own." (Schmidt
v. United States, 177 F. 2d 450, 451.)

Hand agrees with Jackson that in these cases the best thing a judge can do is make the best guess he can. "We must own that the statute imposes upon courts a task impossible of assured execution; people differ as much about moral conduct as they do about beauty. There is not the slightest doubt that to many thousands of our citizens nothing will excuse any sexual irregularity; for some indeed this extends even to the subsequent marriage of an innocent divorced spouse. On the other hand, there are many thousands who look with a complaisant eye upon putting an easy end to one union and taking on another. Our duty in such cases, as we understand it, is to divine what the 'common conscience' prevalent at the time demands; and it is impossible in practice to ascertain what in a given instance it does demand. We should have no warrant for assuming that it meant the judgment of some ethical elite, even if any criterion were available to select them. Nor is it possible to make use of general principles, for almost every moral situation is unique; and no one could be sure how far the distinguishing features of each case would be morally relevant to one person and not to another. Theoretically, perhaps we might take as the test whether those who would approve the specific conduct would outnumber those who would disapprove; but it would be fantastically absurd to try to apply it. So it seems to us that we are confined to the best guess we can make of how such a poll would result." (*Johnson* v. *United States*, 186 F. 2d 588.)

Is there not something cockeyed, even as a theory, about guessing at the result of a poll which it would be fantastically absurd to take? I'd sooner a judge took the perilous path into the interior, seeking his own notion of what was right and what was wrong. And I have high authority for this. John Chipman Gray, in his *Nature and Sources of Law*, said: "We all agree that many cases should be decided by the courts on notions of right and wrong, and of course everyone will agree that a judge is likely to share the notions of right and wrong prevalent in the community in which he lives; but suppose in a case where there is nothing to guide him but notions of right and wrong, that his notions of right and wrong differ from those of his community. Which ought he to follow—his own notions or the notions of the community? Mr. Carter's theory requires him to say that the judge must follow the notions of the community. I believe that he should follow his own notions."

When the legislature asked the judge to decide, the legislature asked *him* to decide, him and no one else. Congress can shirk its duty. A court cannot. And yet such cases as these are not properly judiciable. The Common Law, with more consideration for judges, perhaps naturally so, allowed them to turn such questions over to a jury, where, it seems to me, they belong. But no, we put these questions of natural law, this natural law that we are talking about, to the judge and expect him to have a ready answer. And not only these questions that belong before a jury but those constitutional questions of due process and the like which, as Brandeis told us, so resemble them, for they too are questions of "what in legal parlance is called a fact, as distinguished from the declaration of a rule of law." (285 U.S. 303.)

The best judges, those who perceive that an attitude of humility serves a useful purpose in these inquiries, are appalled. Frankfurter spoke informally at the annual dinner of the Office of the General Counsel of the Navy a year or so ago. He said:

"Well, in a country *like* ours, a system *like* ours, every question, every question, sooner or later may become—and I am appalled at the number of times it does become—a matter of determination by, ultimately, five men sitting up there in the Supreme Court of the United States. I say I am appalled. And it is no secret to those who follow Supreme Court decisions that there is needed above all a feeling of humility in that post. For myself, I know it is one of the dominating factors in my whole outlook on constitutional law. It is a terrible responsibility to put on any five mortals. And I can assure you that that Court has always been manned by mere mortals. In all events, take my word for it, it is now." (*Federal Bar Journal*, January-March 1958.)

Edmond Cahn, on the other hand, is not disturbed. He is quite willing to have a judge decide for himself by himself. "In executing that responsibility there is little reason to fear that a judge, relying on his own deliberate reflections and the call of his own conscience, will apply erratic, capricious, or idiosyncratic moral standards. Our judges are products of our society, and as Professor Gray noted, they will generally think along with the beliefs of some substantial segment of the citizenry. A man who uses a moral standard that no one shares in a population of 150 million probably does not belong at large, much less on the bench. Irrationality we need hardly fear; we have more cause to fear the making of decisions by a judge who deems himself the mouthpiece of an unidentifiable, amorphous, and irresponsible mass. . . .

"Generally speaking, it is the best and finest of judges who afflict themselves with the whips of doubt while their inferior colleagues remain in a state of complacency. What the community needs most is the moral leadership of such a man as Learned Hand and the full benefit of his mature and chastened wisdom. The community is perhaps not at fault when it calls upon him and those like him to test and determine the good moral character of aliens who wish to join its ranks.

"The path of personal responsibility, thorny though it be, remains the only path anyone has ever found to wise and righteous judgment." ("Authority and Responsibility," *Columbia Law Review*, November 1951.)

This "path of personal responsibility," the only path, Cahn asserts, "anyone has ever found to wise and righteous judgment," turns and twists back to where we came on a farm boy eating apple pie and thinking about the law as a career. Now that we have tossed out revelation and come to know the helplessness of pure reason, we don't know where to turn. We look about, but are we sure that we are not looking at ourselves in a mirror? Man is the measure of all things. Does this include himself?

Hume, at the end of the introduction to his *Treatise of Human Nature,* said, "Moral philosophy has, indeed, this peculiar disadvantage, which is not found in natural, that in collecting its experiments it cannot make them purposely, with premeditation, and after such a manner as to satisfy itself concerning every particular difficulty which may arise. When I am at a loss to know the effects of one body upon another in any situation, I need only put them in that situation, and observe what results from it. But should I endeavor to clear up after the same manner any doubt in moral philosophy, by placing myself in the same case with that which I consider, it is evident this reflection and premeditation would so disturb the operation of my natural principles as must render it impossible to form any just conclusion from the phenomenon. We must, therefore, glean up our experiments in this science from a cautious observation of human life, and take them as they appear in the common course of the world, by men's behavior in company, in affairs, and in their pleasures." (Isaiah Berlin quotes this in his book, *The Age of Enlightenment,* on p. 165; Houghton Mifflin, 1956.)

You see how hard it is to regard this domain of natural law as a government of laws and not of men. It comes even harder to accept what John Dewey said we really had, a government of *lawyers* and not of men. Thomas Reed Powell never forgot hearing Dewey say this, and he remembered it again when he gave the last lectures he ever gave, at Columbia in 1956 (*Vagaries and Varieties in Constitutional Interpretation,* p. 24). Perhaps we are being forced back to a government of men as better, at any rate here, than either a government of law or of lawyers.

I turn to another who knows more about this than we do. Frank-

furter has long insisted that the best Justices are not those who have
had judicial experience but, rather, those who had gathered worldly
wisdom from experience with the world. We are likely to think that a
judge must be a lawyer. All the Justices of the Supreme Court have
been lawyers. At any rate I cannot think of any who were not. But
the Constitution does not say they must be. Someday we may live up
to the freedom of choice our forefathers gave us. Consider what
Frankfurter has said about prior *judicial* experience. (In his Roberts
Memorial Lecture at the University of Pennsylvania Law School in
1957.) He didn't, perhaps he wouldn't, go so far as to welcome a
layman to the Court. I can't say.

Frankfurter pointed out that twenty-eight of the seventy-five
Justices (there have been a couple more since) had never sat on the
bench, and who were they? It will take a lawyer to appreciate their
significance. I give you half of them: Marshall, Story, Taney, Curtis,
Miller, Chase, Bradley, Waite, Fuller, Moody, Hughes, Brandeis,
Stone, Roberts, and for good measure I'll add, not on his authority,
Frankfurter himself. He concludes, "One is entitled to say without
qualification that the co-relation between prior judicial experience and
fitness for the functions of the Supreme Court is zero."

If a Justice is no better for having been a judge, how much better is
he for still being a lawyer, anyhow in these wide-open spaces where
our natural law is the only law there is? And where, as Black believed,
you recall, the Court "roams at will in the limitless area of their own
beliefs." I don't think we so much mind their roaming as we do their
settling down somewhere in permanent residence. A judge ought not
to settle down. He does best as a sojourner or a commorant, and most
judges like it best. There is still something of the circuit rider left in
judges. They're not vagrants. Vagrancy is just as disquieting to the
orderly mind as power is corrupting of the ambitious, and judges are
by nature tidy-minded. I am more fearful of our judges settling down
than I am of their roaming.

X

WE TOOK a departure from a bearing on a headland in Hand's lectures. We should now be making a landfall.

Hand did not discuss "whether it might not be desirable to have a third chamber." "I shall assume for argument that it would be." I'll go further. I believe that it is even more than desirable, in fact indispensable, that there be someone to interpret this natural component of law to us, translate it into speech, lift it out of the tacit and the implicit, make it articulate. This is what the Court is doing, as we have seen, when it acts as a third chamber.

It has been well said that the great irony of our time is the way the welfare state, as it undertakes to do more and more and take more and more responsibility for its citizens, loses their loyalty, and that the great riddle of today is how to regain it. The answer, I think, is as human and homely as the answer Oedipus gave the Sphinx, which was simply Man.

We often make the mistake of thinking of loyalty as something owed or paid to a superior, here loyalty to the state, which, in the case of the welfare state we may even confuse with gratitude, such as we owe to a parent. A better analogy would be the responsibility we feel for a child, for the state is more truly our child than our parent. However, the loyalty we seek here is not loyalty to the state but loyalty to each other. As we require the state to do more and more for us, we must relieve the state by making more of our law for ourselves; and this, after all, is no more, no less, than what we have been calling natural law.

If a thing goes without saying, it goes the better for being said. Likewise natural law needs a prophet. The natural law which permeated and pervaded our society in the eighteenth century was none the worse for those ubiquitous verities and all the better for being more specifically expressed in the Bill of Rights. Benjamin F. Wright, in his Bacon lectures last year, had a happy word for our natural law then: *consensus*. Professor Wright said:

"Perhaps the most important product of this long experience in self-government was consensus. If I seem to belabor this concept, it is because we have so long taken it for granted, and because it has sometimes been obscured by the efforts of historians to trace the outlines of class conflict in this period of our past. But the consensus was there, and it was crucial. Moreover, it was not the consensus of ideology, or desperation, or crisis, or any other that may temporarily unite a people revolting against a specific evil. It was rather the consensus rooted in the common life, habits, institutions, and experience of generations. And furthermore, it was the consensus of contentment and success, not misery and oppression. It was therefore durable and flexible, associated with community self-confidence and conducive to moderation."

It is this consensus, which, I take it, is what I have been calling natural law, that justifies the assertion that the best government is the one that governs least. For the truth, and the only truth, in that adage lies in its converse—that the more we govern each other, the less government we need. Freedom from the need of positive law, freedom from the authority of the state—what is this but freedom to govern ourselves? And what is that but governing each other, in our lodges, unions, jobs, churches, families, street gangs, clubs, and neighborhoods? There is no absolute freedom this side of MacLeish's inward country where there is no law. The only freedom in the country of law is a diversity of servitudes.

XI

WE HAVE MADE our landfall, and we are now coming into port.

Do we want the Supreme Court to be the prophet of our natural law? Is the courthouse the right building for the stone? Let me put it this way—Could we persuade Hand to accept the Court as a third legislative chamber? I doubt it. Let us try. Here are Hand's objections:

The first is that a judicial third legislative chamber—which is what Hand now takes it the Court is—does not accord with "the underlying presuppositions of popular government." No, it does not. The Court is an aristocratic enclave. But who said we wanted to take our democracy straight? Why can't we have just enough aristocracy to starch our intellectual collars and keep a crease in our emotional pants?

The Court is "unaccountable to anyone but itself." Unaccountable, yes; except that the Court gives elaborate, sometimes even too elaborate, reasons for its decisions; and, as we have seen, to a large and important extent—just where Holmes thought it most important—though the Court may not be accountable, it is controllable by Congress.

Then Hand says this: "Nothing, I submit, could warrant such a censorship except a code of paramount law that not only measured the scope of legislative authority but regulated how it should be exercised."

To be sure, we have no code of paramount law. We have shuffled off the natural law of St. Thomas Aquinas and the all-too-rational natural law of Thomas Jefferson. Though we have no paramount law, I think it is clear that we have in Congress a paramount legislator. Will not this serve Hand's purpose?

Finally we come to an objection no one is more competent to make than Hand, both as a judge himself and as a member of that society of craftsmen, called the Society of Jobbists, which Holmes founded and of which Hand is now the President. This objection, in Hand's words, is this: "Besides, for a judge to serve as a communal mentor appears to me a very dubious addition to his duties and one apt to interfere with their proper discharge."

The Court's authority, you will recall, for the performance of these duties is their necessity "to prevent the failure of the undertaking." The Court's power, therefore, is strictly confined "to the need that evoked it"—that is, the need that the several States, the Congress, the President, and the Court itself, each keeps within its own "frontiers" and does not "overstep the borders of its authority."

The Court is performing two distinct but practically indistinguishable functions. One is of the highest necessity: "to prevent the failure of the undertaking," the one for which the Court is "undoubtedly the best 'Department' in which to vest such a power." The other is the role of "a communal mentor," a third legislative chamber. Plainly this legislative function should not be permitted to interfere with the successful performance of a role that is necessary to prevent the failure of the undertaking.

Just as this power to keep Congress, the President, and the States within their constitutional bounds springs from necessity and not from anything said in the Constitution, so the force and the effectiveness with which the Court exercises it spring from the Court's prestige and the respect owed and paid to the Court by the other departments, Congress in particular. It is this same prestige and respect which leaves the Court so free to legislate under the Fourteenth Amendment, the Commerce Clause, and in the other ways that we have discussed. The Court relies on this prestige and this respect for the successful and effective performance of both functions, both the indispensable arbiter of the separation of powers and the legislator by leave of Congress. What hurts one detracts from the other.

So long as the Court permits itself, or Congress permits the Court, to legislate so freely on controversial subjects and with such an air of finality, the Court's prestige and authority are expended and hazarded for a purpose that may be useful but is certainly not necessary, the less well and the less effectively will the Court be able to exercise its indispensable function.

Let the Court stop doubling in brass. It has a part to perform. Let it stop playing in the band and step up on the stage where it belongs. A dozen years ago, when Hand spoke at the 250th anniversary of our Supreme Judicial Court, at Boston in 1942, he said:

"These stately admonitions . . . are the precipitates of 'old, unhappy, far-off things, and battles long ago,' originally cast as universals to enlarge the scope of the victory, to give it authority, to reassure the very victors themselves that they have been champions in something more momentous than a passing struggle. Thrown large upon the screen of the future as eternal verities, they are emptied of the vital occasions which gave them birth and become moral adjurations, the more imperious because inscrutable, but with only that content which each generation must pour into them anew in the light of its own experience. If an independent judiciary seeks to fill them from its own bosom, in the end it will cease to be independent. And its independence will be well lost, for that bosom is not ample enough for the hopes and fears of all sorts and conditions of men, nor will its answers be theirs; it must be content to stand aside from these fateful battles. There are two ways in which the judges may forfeit their independence, if they do not abstain. If they are intransigent but honest, they will be curbed; but a worse fate will befall them if they learn to trim their sails to the prevailing winds. A society whose judges have taught it to expect complaisance will exact complaisance; and complaisance under the pretense of interpretation is rottenness. If judges are to kill this thing they love, let them do it, not like cowards with a kiss, but like brave men with a sword.

"And so, to sum up, I believe that for by far the greater part of their work it is a condition upon the success of our system that the judges should be independent; and I do not believe that their independence should be impaired because of their constitutional function. But the price of this immunity, I insist, is that they should not have the last word in those basic conflicts of 'right and wrong—between whose endless jar justice resides.'" (*The Spirit of Liberty*, ed. by Irving Dilliard, Knopf; pp. 163-4.)

This is why I am sure we shall fail to persuade Hand to accept the Supreme Court as a third legislative chamber, or, as I put it, the prophet of our natural law. And this is why, try as hard as I can to persuade myself that Hand is wrong, I believe he is right.

I have left out of account, as best I could, the fact that Learned Hand is the nearest thing we have to the bevy of the Platonic Guardians he scoffs at and says he would find so irksome, and which he would not choose even if he knew how. All we have done is examine what he said, taking nothing, so far as I can recall, on faith or for granted; and I, for one, agree with him.

XII

H AND IS WILLING to "take our chances that such constitutional restraints as already exist may not sufficiently arrest the recklessness of popular assemblies." What I have been saying comes, I think, to much the same thing. I am leaving, and leaving very reluctantly, our natural law to take its chances without a national prophet.

It may be better so. I don't know. Would God that all the Lord's people were prophets, just as the Lord told Moses that the Children of Israel would be unto him a kingdom of priests! I comfort my thoughts by what Hand also told us in Massachusetts when we were celebrating the 250th anniversary of our Court: "In a society which evades its responsibility by thrusting upon the courts the nurture of the spirit of moderation, that spirit in the end will perish." I feel helpless, and I wonder.

What do you say to a Joint Committee of Congress? The Joint Committee on Atomic Energy seems to be doing a good job. What do you say to Congress' raising the prophet's mantle from the shoulders of the Court and throwing it over the shoulders of, say, a Joint Committee of Congress on Spiritual Energy? This would be a practical as well as an inevitable climax to the process along which Congress is reaching an appreciation of its authority over the Court's exercise of legislative powers.

READER: "Isn't that a rather silly title?"

Perhaps so. But at all costs we must keep alive the aspirations of the Thirty-ninth Congress which later Congresses lost. If Congress is going to take back and do what the Court has been doing for two generations, we must make as certain as we can that Congress takes over the emotional earnestness which has led us to think the Court was performing this legislative role, not as a stand-in, but in its own right. I am thinking of the fervor, for example, with which Cardozo expressed the Court's feelings about rights which were "implicit in the concept of ordered liberty," of the generous eloquence that runs through so many of the Court's opinions on due process of law and the equal protection of the laws. Read again Black's moving opinion in the *Chambers* case. Frankfurter's plea for what I regard as a natural law for today does not lack passion, nor does Black's preference for our traditional rights lack a prophetic eagerness. Warren's calm simple statement of our equal rights in public education had none the less fire in its belly.

XIII

READER: "I am more interested in your proposals than in their enthusiasms. If the Court is no longer to be the prophet of our natural law, won't the Court lose much, even all of the prestige on which its power so largely rests?"

It will never come to that. What I am proposing is a process of definition by Congress, which will bit by bit reduce the area in which the Court is now left to its own devices. Anyone who applies general language to particular events is more or less on his own. If he has no one to turn to, he may very well throw up his hands and decline the responsibility. We saw four of the Justices do just that, when they were given nothing but the phrase *moral turpitude* as an index for deportation. The more Congress says what it means, the less the Court will have to tell Congress what it ought to have meant, but Congress will never make the law specific enough to do without some sort or other of natural law. There will always remain enough natural law in the law to give the Court at least the prestige of a minor prophet. In particular, there is all the natural law in which and on which our constitutional rights stand. More than other rights, they arise in concrete circumstances, and this calls for judicial handling. Legislatures deal only with generalities, as indeed they must, since they are providing for the future. Only courts can handle the particular and actual cases in which justice is made flesh.

Our courts will continue to be at least the minor prophets of our
natural law, and that is prestige enough for a court. I see no reason
why any court, however supreme, should be an oracle, like Delphi,
Dordona, or Bacbuc, as who say, "I am Sir Oracle, and when I ope
my lips, let no dog bark." There's an odor of hugger-muggery about
an oracle that ill suits the dignity of a court. As arbiter between the
organs of our government, the separator, if I may put it so, of the
powers of our government, an esteem based on impartiality will make
the Court's opinions far more persuasive than any amount of oracular
awe. I should like to see the Court come out from behind the reredos,
down from the mountain, up out of the cave, and stop indulging our
illusion that statesmanship is law, and vice versa.

We used to think of our Supreme Court as a court of law. No one,
except those prejudiced in favor of the law or those who are ignorant
of everything else, would think this now. You recall the judge who
told Holmes that he never made a decision unless he was absolutely
sure that it was right. There was emblazoned, or at least framed, in
his mind what Lord Chief Justice Coke told James the First when he
tried to meddle with the law. Coke told James that the King was *sub
Deo et lege,* under God and the Law. The fortunes of the King's
subjects, Coke explained, "were not to be decided by natural reason
but by the artificial reason and judgment of law, which law is an art
which requires long study and experience before that a man can attain
to the cognizance of it." (12 *Coke's Reports* 64, 65.)

"Under God and the Law!" has been the device of lawyers from
one generation to another ever since Coke's colloquy with the King
in 1608. It is chiseled in stone along the face of Langdell Hall in the
Harvard Law School. This is not the place to discuss trust in God,
but we are learning that the Law has no longer all the answers.

We must reconcile ourselves to the fact that the Court has become
much more than a court of law. Ninety-odd per cent of the cases filed
with the clerk are being heard only at the Court's discretion. They are

filed as petitions for *certiorari*, and the Court grants or denies the petition without a hearing. How does the Court choose? What sort of case does the Court cull out—about one in five—for a hearing and a decision on its merits? Not those in which justice seems to have been most offended. It is the established policy of the Court to choose "in the interest of the law, its appropriate exposition and enforcement, not in the mere interest of the litigants." I am quoting Chief Justice Hughes, who was in turn quoted by Justice John M. Harlan, when he gave the Cardozo Lecture to the Association of the Bar of the City of New York in the fall of 1958. (*The Record* for December 1958 ran the whole address.)

Justice Harlan summed it up this way: "The Supreme Court is not a court of errors and appeals in the same sense as most highest state courts. A federal litigant whose case has been through the district court and then the Court of Appeals is deemed to have had his 'day in court,' so far as the case involves merely the private interests of the parties. If further review is to be had by the Supreme Court it must be because of the public interest in the questions involved."

What kind of a law court ignores "the mere interest of the litigants" and concerns itself only with "the public interest in the questions involved"? Our Supreme Court has all but ceased to be a court of law in any ordinary sense and become, under stress of our expectations, something more like an inferior legislature, carrying on where Congress left off.

Harlan was deploring the glut of petitions for *certiorari*—that is, for leave to have your case heard by the Court—as "an aspect of one of the great problems confronting the administration of justice in this country today—namely, how are the courts to keep on top of their ever-increasing work load?" He is thinking, of course, of his own, the Supreme Court of the United States, and so are we here. I make no doubt of the importance of the problem. The more you must do, the less you can think. A hurried court is no court at all. Unless justice is deliberate, it is not judicial. That the Justices should "keep on top of their ever-increasing work load" is not enough. We want the Court to have time to think, leisure to reflect, space in which to contemplate. Harrison Tweed once told me that every law office that could afford it ought to have a partner who did nothing but live the contemplative life, contemplating the possibilities inherent in the other partners' doings which they were too busy to perceive. How much more wise and true this is of the Court! We could very well count it a blessing if the Court had time for contemplation as well as deliberation.

XIV

THE JUSTICES TALK TOO MUCH, and it is our fault that they do. We are simple-minded enough to expect the Court to legislate with unanimity, even on the most controversial subjects, and we are surprised that the Justices do not always agree. It is naïve of us. It is also discreditable to expect conscientious judges to sink their consciences out of respect for the prestige of the Court. You recall the old adage: he who insists on never being wrong had better keep silent. Our Justices are wise enough, clear-headed enough, to know that they can never be sure they are right. So, of course, they talk too much. So long as we ask the Court to legislate as well as adjudicate, we must not only expect, we must welcome, dissenting and concurring opinions. Justice Douglas has told us why this must be so. He was speaking to the Section on Judicial Administration of the American Bar Association (September 8, 1948; *Journal of the American Judicature Society* for December 1948) :

"Democracy, like religion, is full of sects and schisms. Every political campaign demonstrates it. Every session of a legislature proves it. No man or group of men has a monopoly on truth, wisdom, or virtue. An idea, once advanced for public acceptance, divides like an amoeba. The if's and but's and however's each claim a part; and what was once a whole is soon carved into many separate pieces, some of which are larger than the original itself.

"Those who have followed the legislative process can produce examples on end. That process is one of compromise—of qualifying absolutes, of creating exceptions to general rules. At times the process of compromise or conciliation involves well-nigh impossible adjustments. The clash of ideas may be so violent that a meeting of the minds seems out of the question. Where such cleavage is great and involves major issues, it may even tear a society apart. By the same token it can stop the legislative process or render it impotent, and thus deprive society of lawful and nonviolent means and methods of solving its problems. When the breach between the pros and cons is not too great, the legislative process functions. Even then, the compromise between competing ideas that emerges in the final legislation may be more apparent than real. For the legislative solution is often to write two opposing ideas into a statute. Without that solution enactment of the measure might, indeed, be impossible.

"And so the bill becomes the law and the law arrives before judges for interpretation. The battle that raged before the legislature is now transferred to the court. The passage of the legislation quieted the conflict only temporarily. It breaks out anew in the process of interpretation in the courts. A storm hits the courtroom, and the advocates take up the fight where the legislators left off. The same cleavage that appeared in legislative halls now shows up among the judges. Each side has eminent authority for its view since two conflicting ideas found their way into the legislation. It is therefore easy for judge or lawyer or editor to accuse the judge who takes the opposing view of usurping the role of the legislature. A more honest, a more objective view would concede that interpretation has legislative as well as judicial characteristics. It cannot be otherwise where the legislature has left the choice of competing theories or ideas to the judges."

You see, it comes down to a question of thrift. The Court is squandering its time and attention on what Congress can do better. How much time would be saved if Congress were to relieve the Court of the legislating that Congress should do, and if it were to do, would do better than the Court! All you can say is that if the Court were as truly a court of law as it has to pretend to be, and as most of its admirers think it is, and as many of its critics wish it were, then the Court could snatch—this is not the right word—a little time from business and devote it to the contemplative life.

In the old days, dissents were rare. When the New Deal split the Court, dissenting became a duty, not only justified but enjoyed by a deep divergence of attitude. After that came the era Douglas was speaking of, when it became a habit. Dissents ran up as high as 80 per cent in 1951. Since then, whether through self-restraint or simple reticence I do not know, dissents receded. You find them now in not much more than half the decisions.

But the point I make is not the number of dissents but the number of dissenting and concurring opinions they inspire, which require as much time and attention as an opinion for the Court. At any rate, some do, and they all ought to. In the term of court of 1957-1958, the Court sent down 119 opinions, and the Justices, singly or in groups, filed 116 more concurring or dissenting opinions, almost as many again. (*Harvard Law Review* for November 1958.) A spot check over the last couple of years shows that these occupied nearly as many of the pages of the reports as the opinions of the majority for the Court. So something like nearly half of the Justices' time and attention was spent in expressing their personal opinions, concurring or dissenting.

How much of this valuable time the Justices will save if they refrain from publishing their legislative debates is beyond guessing. Do not forget that each Justice is as independent as a conscientious man can be. He is as independent of the Court as the Court is independent of Congress or the President. But if the Justices are as wise for their own account as they are for others, which would be scarcely human, they will spend the time they save by ceasing to act like a third legislative chamber on those high matters in which by general acclaim we expect them to act, keeping the different departments of our government, including the Court itself, from stepping on each other's toes. This is the arbitrament of the separation of powers, which Hand says is "necessary to prevent the failure of the under-taking." "Without some arbiter whose decision should be final," he said, "the whole system would have collapsed."

We are a democracy with an appallingly successful record over a span of half a dozen generations, old enough, as nations go, to worry about our age. A democracy, yes; but out of caution our founders hedged their trust in the common people by separating the powers of popular government. They created a democracy less capable of destroying itself, at the price of making it less capable of becoming a great nation in a troubled world. And the Court, by general acclaim, has undertaken to see to it that this unstable equilibrium of separate and yet kindred powers, legislative, executive, and judicial, is maintained.

"The courts," Hand said, "were undoubtedly the best 'Department' in which to vest such a power, since by the independence of their tenure they were least likely to be influenced by diverting pressure." But independence does not assure success. Wisdom and the accouterments of wisdom are as essential to the success of this arbitrament between the departments, including, mind you, the Court itself, as its success is "necessary to prevent the failure of the undertaking."

The Court is here working in such an exalted sphere that it can expect little or no help from the law. There are no precedents here to turn to. Indeed, the word *precedent* becomes ungainly and contradictory in these matters. For a precedent is something in the past that we follow, and so we back into the future, which is not at all the right attitude. Here the Court must face the future. What matters here is wisdom, and what the Court must rely on here is the power of persuasion. Authority has been left behind. We expect the Justices to be wise men, statesmen, politicians *in excelsis.*

Success depends on two things. One is our good sense. The other is the excellence of the Court's advice. The Justices have to rely on us for the first. For the other, they must turn to the ancient sources, those two accouterments of wisdom, meditation and discussion, sometimes more of one, sometimes more of the other, always much of both, first one, then the other, and repeat.

As you see, we have reached another frontier of law. Just as we looked across the marches into MacLeish's inward country, now we stand at the frontier between law and statesmanship. When we ask our Court to act as arbiter between the three departments of our government, we are asking the Justices to go beyond law, into a country where there are no precedents and very little dogma to help their judgment. Here they are unavoidably statesmen and not lawyers, just as in MacLeish's inward country we are not lawyers but individualists. There Thoreau is the patron saint. Here it must be Lincoln, who was our greatest constitutional lawyer because he was never under the illusion that it was law.

We had a glimpse at the inward country. Before I put up the shutters, I will give you a glimpse from far off of the kind of thing we ask the Court to do here.

In 1952 President Truman seized most of the nation's steel mills and directed Charles Sawyer, the Secretary of Commerce, to operate them. The reason for the seizure was a labor dispute which the United Steel Workers and the steel mills were unable to settle. On April 4, 1952, the union gave notice of a nation-wide strike to begin on April 9. On the eighth the President seized the mills and at the same time sent a message to Congress asking that Congress do something to meet this emergency which would stop the production of steel and jeopardize the national defense. This was in the midst of our war in Korea.

These are facts enough for our purpose, for I am not going to ask you to match your judgment against the Court, which held, six to three, that the President, under the circumstances, in view of all that Congress had said and had not said, had no power to seize the mills. (*Youngstown Sheet and Tube Co.* v. *Sawyer*, 343 U.S. 579.)

The first thing I want to point out is that each of the Justices wrote his own separate opinion, concurring with Black's opinion for the Court or dissenting. I want you to agree with me that Frankfurter's comment was just and wise: "Even though such differences in attitude toward this principle [the separation of powers] may be merely differences in emphasis and nuance, they can hardly be reflected by a single opinion for the Court. Individual expression of views reaching a common result is therefore important." I ask you also to agree that the three Justices who dissented were involuntarily paying tribute when they said: "The diversity of views expressed in the seven opinions of the majority, the lack of reference to authoritative precedent, the repeated reliance upon prior dissenting opinions, the complete disregard of the uncontroverted facts showing the gravity of the emergency and the temporary nature of the taking all serve to demonstrate how far afield one must go to affirm the order of the District Court which enjoined the seizure as unconstitutional and unauthorized."

Now a quick look at the kind of statesmanship we expect of the Court in this far country. I can give you the account of a participant in it as well as a judge of it. Here are the first three paragraphs of Jackson's concurring opinion:

"That comprehensive and undefined presidential powers hold both practical advantages and grave dangers for the country will impress anyone who has served as legal adviser to a President in time of transition and public anxiety. While an interval of detached reflection may temper teachings of that experience, they probably are a more realistic influence on my views than the conventional materials of judicial decision which seem unduly to accentuate doctrine and legal fiction. But as we approach the question of presidential power, we half overcome mental hazards by recognizing them. The opinions of judges, no less than executives and publicists, often suffer the infirmity of confusing the issue of a power's validity with the cause it is invoked to promote, of confounding the permanent executive office with its temporary occupant. The tendency is strong to emphasize transient results upon policies—such as wages or stabilization—and lose sight of enduring consequences upon the balanced power structure of our Republic.

"A judge, like an executive adviser, may be surprised at the poverty of really useful and unambiguous authority applicable to concrete problems of executive power as they actually present themselves. Just what our forefathers did envision, or would have envisioned had they foreseen modern conditions, must be divined from materials almost as enigmatic as the dreams Joseph was called upon to interpret for Pharaoh. A century and a half of partisan debate and scholarly speculation yields no net result but only supplies more or less apt quotations from respected sources on each side of any question. They largely cancel each other. And court decisions are indecisive because of the judicial practice of dealing with the largest questions in the most narrow way.

"The actual art of governing under our Constitution does not and cannot conform to judicial definitions of the power of any of its branches based on isolated clauses or even single Articles torn from context. While the Constitution diffuses power the better to secure liberty, it also contemplates that practice will integrate the dispersed powers into a workable government. It enjoins upon its branches separateness but interdependence, autonomy but reciprocity. Presidential powers are not fixed but fluctuate, depending upon their disjunction or conjunction with those of Congress. . . ."

XV

WHAT, THEN, after all, are we to think of our Supreme Court?

I am encouraged by a verse I read the other day, No. 59 of 95 *Poems* by E. E. Cummings:

> when any mortal (even the most odd)
>
> can justify the ways of man to God
> i'll think it strange that normal mortals can
>
> not justify the ways of God to man

And I will not be discouraged by John Milton's attempt.

To me, the spectacular thing about the Court is the wonderful variety of jobs we ask it to do for us, and the Court's even more wonderful willingness to undertake them. Our Johannes Factotum; indeed, the Pooh-Bah of our government. For was not the Court persuaded to be the Lord High Executioner of the New Deal, back in 1935 and 1936?

We have watched the Court relieving Congress of the burden of enforcing the Fourteenth Amendment. We have seen the President, as if it were his duty, expect the Court, and not he, to take care that the law desegregating our public schools be faithfully executed.

116

Indeed, the President has not even expressed his opinion on this, the greatest moral issue of his era (August 21 and 27, 1958; and January 21, 1959). If he approves, should he not say so? If he disapproves, should he not ask Congress to correct the Court, as plainly it could, under Section Five of the Fourteenth Amendment, by putting us back to "separate but equal" schools? Is the Court the only department of our government carrying the courage of the Constitution?

All this, if you please, the Court is doing on top of its regular occupation, interpreting acts of Congress, clearing up the several jurisdictions of the administrative agencies, straightening out the conflicting rulings of the circuit courts, and acting as the final court of appeals in patent cases, admiralty, and Federal taxation, to say nothing of all the et cetera. And—let me speak feelingly as a lawyer—I hope the Court will never quite lose all interest in private litigation. Let it now and then burn a candle to the Goddess by deciding disputes that are important only to the parties. Let the Court never lose the judicial touch! Justice, as well as politics, has its grass roots.

The other thing about the Court is not at all spectacular. Usually people excel by reason of some special talent or by a proficiency in some specialized craft or skill, but the thing about the Court seems to me to be that a good Justice needs no special talent or skill. We turn to the Court and we respect the Court's opinions just because it is not a specialist, either in the law or in anything else in particular. The Justices, nine of them, are blessed with intelligence, bred in experience, human and hard. They have been ambitious, but now they are thinking, not about themselves, but about others. Where they sit, ambition has ceased to be a virtue. Some of them become altruistic. Others rise above that to vicariousness. There is nothing at all parental about them, but they are not too remote to be avuncular. They gather and discuss, agree or disagree, above the noise of the traffic. They are spectators who have been participants, philosophers who were once practitioners. In an era of specialists, the Justices make sagacity their business.

I don't know how to give you an idea of the variety of the doubts and queries we thrust at the Court; nor of their difficulty, except to say that the problems others put up to you are likely to be the hard ones. Let me put all this in a roundabout way. Some people live mainly in the present. This is the simplest, and may be the best. It is the Legislative life, where our demands congregate and our troubles are most insistent. Others live mainly in the past, where passions are spent and can be relived only in effigy or in awe. And there are those who live mainly in the future and save their awe for what's to come. They are our leaders, whatever office they happen to hold. Only the Judiciary, only the Court, spans and unites all three with its attention—the past, the present, and the future. This is why we turn so often, so insistently, and, yes, gratefully to the Court with our doubts, our queries, and our insoluble problems. For only the Court knows how to bring the past up close enough to touch the outstretched finger of the future, and yet not so close as to tread on its heels. Only the Court in our Government knows that this is a relay race.

SUPPLEMENT

I HAVE PUT HERE, in a supplement, some things I feared the reader would not skip if they were in the text.

They bear in one way or another upon what we have been discussing, but in the text they would have been digressions, diversions, or countervailing considerations. In other words, they would be obstacles, I thought, to a continuous understanding.

The most important are discussions and explanations of some of the ways to approach an understanding of what I am calling "natural law." I put it in quotation marks to make it quite clear that the phrase is a tag. It does not pretend to be a definition, nor even descriptive; nor are these discussions and explanations. But they may bring us closer to a fix of our understanding by coming from different directions.

❧ Supplementary to page 11.

One approach to what I am calling natural law is by way of Whitehead's distinction between immanent and imposed law. In his *Adventures of Ideas*, he says, "By the doctrine of Law as immanent it is meant that the order of nature expresses the characters of the real things which jointly compose the existences to be found in nature.

121

When we understand the essences of these things, we thereby know their mutual relations to each other. Thus, according as there are common elements in their various characters, there will necessarily be corresponding identities in their mutual relations. In other words, some partial identity of pattern in the various characters of natural things issues in some partial identity of pattern in the mutual relations of those things. These identities of pattern in the mutual relations are the Laws of Nature. Conversely, a Law is explanatory of some community in character pervading the things which constitute Nature. It is evident that the doctrine involves the negation of 'absolute being.' It presupposes the essential interdependence of things."

This doctrine, Whitehead goes on to say, carries consequences with it. "The exact conformation of nature to any law is not to be expected. If all the things concerned have the requisite common character, then the pattern of mutual relevance which expresses that character will be exactly illustrated. But in general we may expect that a large proportion of things do possess the requisite character and a minority do not possess it. In such a case, the mutual relations of these things will exhibit lapses when the law fails to obtain illustration."

Moreover, "since the laws of nature depend on the individual character of things constituting nature, as the things change, then correspondingly the laws will change. . . . Thus the conception of the Universe as evolving subject to fixed, eternal laws regulating all behavior should be abandoned."

Whitehead contrasts an Imposed Order. "The doctrine of Imposed Law adopts the alternative metaphysical doctrine of External Relations between the Existences which are the ultimate constituents of nature. The character of each of these ultimate things is thus conceived as its own private qualification. Such an existent is understandable in complete disconnection from any other such existent: the ultimate truth is that it requires nothing but itself in order to exist. But in fact there is imposed on each such existent the necessity of entering into relationships with the other ultimate constituents of nature. These imposed behavior patterns are the Laws of Nature. But you cannot discover the natures of the relata by any study of the Laws of their relations. Nor, conversely, can you discover the laws by inspection of the natures."

"The Laws of Nature" of which Whitehead is here speaking is not our natural law. They are the laws of physical nature that scientists seek and lawyers know nothing about. But the distinction between science and the humanities is not so deep as some humanists think, and the *difference* between an immanent and an imposed law seems to me to be precisely the same as the *difference* between a natural law in our sense and the positive law.

Another approach is from symbolism. Charles S. Peirce said, "A Symbol incorporates a habit, and is indispensable to the application of any *intellectual* habit, at least." This is in the fourth volume of Peirce's *Collected Papers,* and I have not read the context. Peirce also said that the meaning of a sign was best described in terms of "the habit which it is calculated to produce." (W. B. Gallie's little book on *Peirce and Pragmatism,* Pelican; p. 129.)

These two cryptic remarks lead us to the third of Whitehead's lectures at the University of Virginia in 1927 on Symbolism. Here is most of it:

"My main thesis is that a social system is kept together by the blind force of instinctive actions, and of instinctive emotions clustered around habits and prejudices. It is therefore not true that any advance in the scale of culture inevitably tends to the preservation of society. On the whole, the contrary is more often the case, and any survey of nature confirms this conclusion. A new element in life renders in many ways the operation of the old instincts unsuitable. But unexpressed instincts are unanalyzed and blindly felt. Disruptive forces, introduced by a higher level of existence, are then warring in the dark against an invisible enemy. There is no foothold for the intervention of 'rational consideration'—to use Henry Osborn Taylor's admirable phrase. The symbolic expression of instinctive forces drags them out into the open: it differentiates them and delineates them. There is then opportunity for reason to effect, with comparative speed, what otherwise must be left to the slow operation of the centuries amid ruin and reconstruction. Mankind misses its opportunities, and its failures are a fair target for ironic criticism. But the fact that reason too often fails does not give fair ground for the hysterical conclusion that it never succeeds. Reason can be compared to the force of gravitation, the weakest of all natural forces, but in the end the creator of suns and of stellar systems—those great societies of the Universe. Symbolic expression first preserves society by adding emotion to instinct, and secondly it affords a foothold for reason by its delineation of the particular instinct which it expresses. This doctrine of the disruptive tendency due to novelties, even those involving a rise to finer levels, is illustrated by the effect of Christianity on the stability of the Roman Empire. It is also illustrated by the three revolutions which secured liberty and equality for the world—namely, the English revolutionary period of the seventeenth century, the American Revolution, and the French Revolution. England barely escaped a disruption of its social system; America was never in any such danger; France, where the entrance of novelty was most intense, did for a time experience this collapse. Edmund Burke, the Whig statesman of the eighteenth century, was the philosopher who was the approving prophet of the two earlier revolutions, and the denunciatory prophet of the French Revolution. A man of genius and a statesman, who has immediately observed two revolutions and has meditated deeply on a third, deserves to be heard when he speaks on the forces which bind and disrupt societies. Unfortunately statesmen are swayed by the passions of the moment, and Burke shared this defect to the full, so as to be carried away by the reactionary passions aroused by the French Revolution. Thus the wisdom of his general conception of social forces is smothered by the wild unbalanced conclusions which he drew from them: his greatness is best shown by his attitude toward the American Revolution. His more general reflections are contained, first, in his youthful work *A Vindication of Natural Society*, and, secondly, in his *Reflections on the French Revolution*. The earlier work was meant ironically; but, as is often the case with genius, he prophesied unknowingly. This essay is practically written round the thesis that advances in the art of civilization are apt to be destructive of the social system. Burke conceived this conclusion to be a *reductio ad absurdum*. But it is the truth. The second work —a work which in its immediate effect was perhaps the most harmful ever written—directs attention to the importance of 'prejudice' as a binding social force. There again I hold that he was right in his premises and wrong in his conclusions.

"Burke surveys the standing miracle of the existence of an organized society, culminating in the smooth unified action of the state. Such a society may consist of millions of individuals, each with its individual character, its individual aims, and its individual selfishness. He asks what is the force which leads this throng of separate units to co-operate in the maintenance of an organized state, in which each individual has his part to play—political, economic, and aesthetic. He contrasts the complexity of the functionings of a civilized society with the sheer diversities of its individual citizens considered as a mere group or crowd. His answer to the riddle is that the magnetic force is 'prejudice,' or, in other words, 'use and wont.' Here he anticipates the whole modern theory of 'herd psychology,' and at the same time deserts the fundamental doctrine of the Whig party, as formed in the seventeenth century and sanctioned by Locke. This conventional Whig doctrine was that the state derived its origin from an 'original contract' whereby the mere crowd voluntarily organized itself into a society. Such a doctrine seeks the origin of the state in a baseless historical fiction. Burke was well ahead of his time in drawing attention to the importance of precedence as a political force. Unfortunately, in the excitement of the moment, Burke construed the importance of precedence as implying the negation of progressive reform.

"Now, when we examine how a society bends its individual members to function in conformity with its needs, we discover that one important operative agency is our vast system of inherited symbolism. There is an intricate expressed symbolism of language and of act, which is spread throughout the community, and which evokes fluctuating apprehension of the basis of common purposes. The particular direction of individual action is directly correlated to the particular sharply defined symbols presented to him at the moment. The response of action to symbol may be so direct as to cut out any effective reference to the ultimate thing symbolized. This elimination of meaning is termed reflex action. Sometimes there does intervene some effective reference to the meaning of the symbol. But this meaning is not recalled with the particularity and definiteness which would yield any rational enlightenment as to the specific action required to secure the final end. The meaning is vague but insistent. Its insistence plays the part of hypnotizing the individual to complete the specific action associated with the symbol. In the whole trans-action, the elements which are clear-cut and definite are the specific symbols and the actions which should issue from the symbols. But in themselves the symbols are barren facts whose direct associative force would be insufficient to procure automatic conformity. There is not sufficient repetition, or sufficient similarity of diverse occasions, to secure mere automatic obedience. But in fact the symbol evokes loyalties to vaguely conceived notions, fundamental for our spiritual natures. The result is that our natures are stirred to suspend all antagonistic impulses, so that the symbol procures its required response in action. Thus the social symbolism has a double meaning. It means pragmatically the direction of individuals to specific action; and it also means theoretically the vague ultimate reasons with their emotional accompaniments, whereby the symbols acquire their power to organize the miscellaneous crowd into a smoothly running community. . . .

"For the greater number of citizens of a state there is in practice no reliable automatic obedience to any symbol such as the word of command for soldiers, except in a few instances such as the response to the signals of the traffic police. Thus the state depends in a very particular way upon the prevalence of symbols which combine direction to some well-known course of action with some deeper reference to the purpose of the state. The self-organization of society depends on commonly diffused symbols evoking commonly diffused ideas, and at the same time indicating commonly understood actions. Usual forms of verbal expression are the most important example of such symbolism. Also the heroic aspect of the history of the country is the symbol for its immediate worth.

"When a revolution has sufficiently destroyed this common symbolism leading to common actions for usual purposes, society can only save itself from dissolution by means of a reign of terror. Those revolutions which escape a reign of terror have left intact the fundamental efficient symbolism of society. For example, the English revolutions of the seventeenth century and the American revolution of the eighteenth century left the ordinary life of their respective communities nearly unchanged. When George Washington had replaced George III, and Congress had replaced the English Parliament, Americans were still carrying on a well-understood system so far as the general structure of their social life was concerned. Life in Virginia must have assumed no very different aspect from that which it had exhibited before the revolution. In Burke's phraseology, the prejudices on which Virginian society depended were unbroken. The ordinary signs still beckoned people to their ordinary actions and suggested the ordinary common-sense justification.

"One difficulty of explaining my meaning is that the intimate effective symbolism consists of the various types of expression which
permeate society and evoke a sense of common purpose. No one
detail is of much importance. The whole range of symbolic expression is required. A national hero, such as George Washington or
Jefferson, is a symbol of the common purpose which animates American life. This symbolic function of great men is one of the difficulties
in obtaining a balanced historical judgment. There is the hysteria of
depreciation, and there is the opposite hysteria which dehumanizes
in order to exalt. It is very difficult to exhibit the greatness without
losing the human being. Yet we know that at least *we* are human
beings; and half the inspiration of our heroes is lost when we forget
that *they* were human beings.

"I mention great Americans, because I am speaking in America.
But exactly the same truth holds for the great men of all countries
and ages. . . .

"Finally, mankind also uses a more artificial symbolism, obtained
chiefly by concentrating on a certain selection of sense-perceptions,
such as words, for example. In this case, there is a chain of deriva-
tions of symbol from symbol whereby finally the local relations,
between the final symbol and the ultimate meaning, are entirely lost.
Thus these derivative symbols, obtained as it were by arbitrary association, are really the results of reflex action suppressing the intermediate portions of the chain. We may use the word *association*
when there is this suppression of intermediate links.

"This derivative symbolism, employed by mankind, is not in general mere indication of meaning, in which every common feature
shared by symbol and meaning has been lost. In every effective symbolism there are certain aesthetic features shared in common. The
meaning acquires emotion and feeling directly excited by the symbol.
This is the whole basis of the art of literature—namely, that emotions
and feelings directly excited by the words should fitly intensify our

emotions and feelings arising from contemplation of the meaning. Further in language there is a certain vagueness of symbolism. A word has a symbolic association with its own history, its other meanings, and with its general status in current literature. Thus a word gathers emotional signification from its emotional history in the past; and this is transferred symbolically to its meaning in present use. . . .

"Thus mankind by means of its elaborate system of symbolic transference can achieve miracles of sensitiveness to a distant environment, and to a problematic future. But it pays the penalty, by reason of the dangerous fact that each symbolic transference may involve an arbitrary imputation of unsuitable characters. It is not true that the mere workings of nature in any particular organism are in all respects favorable either to the existence of that organism, or to its happiness, or to the progress of the society in which the organism finds itself. The melancholy experience of men makes this warning a platitude. No elaborate community of elaborate organisms could exist unless its systems of symbolism were in general successful. Codes, rules of behavior, canons of art, are attempts to impose systematic action which on the whole will promote favorable symbolic interconnections. As a community changes, all such rules and canons require revision in the light of reason. The object to be obtained has two aspects; one is the subordination of the community to the individuals composing it, and the other is the subordination of the individuals to the community. Free men obey the rules which they themselves have made. Such rules will be found in general to impose on society behavior in reference to a symbolism which is taken to refer to the ultimate purposes for which the society exists.

"It is the first step in sociological wisdom to recognize that the major advances in civilization are processes which all but wreck the societies in which they occur—like unto an arrow in the hand of a child. The art of free society consists first in the maintenance of the symbolic code; and secondly in fearlessness of revision, to secure that the code serves those purposes which satisfy an enlightened reason. Those societies which cannot combine reverence to their symbols with freedom of revision must ultimately decay either from anarchy, or from the slow atrophy of a life stifled by useless shadows."

I turn to Ruth Benedict and take a paragraph from her *Patterns of Culture* (p. 252) :

"Society," she says, "is only incidentally and in certain situations regulative, and law is not equivalent to the social order. In the simpler homogeneous cultures collective habit and custom may quite supersede the necessity for any development of formal legal authority. American Indians sometimes say, 'In the old days, there were no fights about hunting grounds or fishing territories. There was no law then, so everybody did what was right.' The phrasing makes it clear that in their old life they did not think of themselves as submitting to a social control imposed upon them from without. Even in our civilization the law is never more than a crude implement of society, and one it is often necessary to check in its arrogant career. It is never to be read off as if it were the equivalent of the social order."

Older readers may exclaim, "William Graham Sumner's *Folkways*, to be sure!" Yes, but Sumner's satisfaction with life and his laissez-faire convictions lead him to regard his folkways in much the same way and with almost as much reverence as St. Thomas Aquinas admired his divine natural law. Let us not make that mistake. Listen to Gunnar Myrdal's comment on Sumner:

"Social scientists are so habituated to using static and fatalistic value premises with such facts as the mores, social processes, and social trends, and they are so prone to associate radical valuation premises with a complete disregard of the facts that they often do not realize that it is quite possible to couple dynamic value premises with factual knowledge of mores, social processes or social trends. The static and fatalistic value premises have actually imbedded themselves into the data. It should not surprise us that the great development of the social sciences in recent decades in America has not been accompanied by a correspondingly important development of social engineering.

"In the theory of folkways and mores the heavy load of do-nothing (*laissez-faire*) valuation becomes particularly apparent when Sumner and his many followers set out with the purpose of proving the inefficacy of legislation. With reference to race relations in the South after the Civil War, Sumner said:

> The two races have not yet made new mores. Vain attempts have been made to control the new order by legislation. The only result is the proof that legislation cannot make mores. . . . It is only just now that the new society seems to be taking shape. There is a trend in the mores now as they begin to form under the new state of things. It is not at all what the humanitarians hoped and expected. . . . Some are anxious to interfere and try to control. They take their stand on ethical views of what is going on. It is evidently impossible for anyone to interfere. We are like spectators at a great natural convulsion. The results will be such as the facts and forces call for. We cannot foresee them. They do not depend on ethical views any more than the volcanic eruption on Martinique contained an ethical element.

"It should be noted that—in spite of its psychologism, its ethical relativism, its modernized terminology, and the abundant anthropological illustrations—this theory is nothing else than a reformulation and slight modification of the old *laissez-faire* doctrine of the 'natural order' as it was more naïvely set forth in the Enlightenment period: human relations are governed by 'natural laws'; 'natural laws' are not only the right laws but are also, in the main, and in spite of all the interferences of foolish governments, actually governing real life; they do not need to be legalized—if legislation adheres to the 'natural laws,' it is not exactly damaging but useless; if legislation conflicts with the 'natural laws' it will be inefficacious though slightly damaging as it will disturb somewhat the smooth operation of the 'natural laws.' This is, for instance, the doctrine behind Adam Smith's well-known dictum that trade barriers, though, of course, irrational and cumbersome, will, by and large, not amount to much, as the smugglers will pierce them, acting here as the agents of the 'natural laws' with the same immutability as water seeking its level. The 'invisible hand' will inevitably guide human activity. On this central point, which apparently is largely the political purpose of the whole theory of folkways and mores, Sumner simply expresses a common American prejudice against legislation which we have discussed."

We, on our part, must not make the mistake of regarding this as a choice between fatalism and free will. On the contrary, these folkways, these patterns, they set us more free, they offer us more freedom. William James told us this secret in his essay on habit: "The more of the details of our daily life we can hand over to the effortless custody of automatism the more our higher powers of mind will be set free for their own proper work." Conformity need no more smother freedom than three meals, a tight roof, and a hot stove strangle individual enterprise.

Dorothy Lee has weighed this delicate antinomy better than anyone I have read. She takes it from a setting where the folkways appear to be omnipotent, and yet individual integrity is cherished and fostered:

"Respect for individual integrity, for what we have called human dignity, has long been a tenet in American culture, and it is certainly no novel principle to anyone working in the area of interpersonal relations. However, in a heterogeneous society such as ours is at present, and in an era of induced change and speeded tempo of living, it has been difficult to implement this tenet in the everyday details of living. We have to reconcile principles of conformity and individual initiative, group living and private freedom of choice, social regulation and personal autonomy. I believe that a study of other societies dealing with such issues in different circumstances can furnish us with insights which we can use in understanding our own situation. So I present here scattered material from a number of societies, ending with a brief sketch of the culture of the Navaho Indians, to show how the principle of personal autonomy is supported by the cultural framework.

"In every society we find some organized social unit; but not everywhere does the social unit provide freedom to the individual or the opportunity for spontaneous functioning; nor do we find everywhere the value for sheer personal being of which I shall speak below. We often find a hierarchy where women or children or the uninitiated or the commoners are accorded a minority status. In some societies we find what amounts to a dictatorship; in others, the group may demand such sacrifice of individual uniqueness as to make for totalitarianism. On the other hand, in some societies we encounter a conception of individual autonomy and democratic procedures which far outstrip anything we have practiced or even have conceived of as democracy. It is only the latter kind which concerns me here. . . .

"Among the Navaho Indians of Arizona and New Mexico, we find a tightly knit group, depending on mutual responsibility among all its members, a precisely structured universe, and a great respect for individual autonomy and integrity. Here we have people who maintain an inviolable privacy while living as a family in a one-room house, sharing work and responsibility to such an extent that even a child of six will contribute his share of mutton to the family meal. The family unit is so closely knit that, if a child of five is ill or absent, the family suffers because there is a gap in the co-operative effort; and when a man goes hunting, he can get nothing unless his wife co-operates at home, by observing the necessary taboos. The well-being of a Navaho, his health and the health of all his undertakings depend on the maintenance of harmony with nature. All being is both good and evil; and by walking carefully according to a highly structured map of procedure, within a detailed framework of 'do's' and 'don't's,' the Navaho can keep the proper balance of good and evil in his life, and thus find health and harmony. The rules according to which he lives originate in the structure and come to him as guidance from the parents, not as commands.

"Within this structured universe and tightly knit society, the Navaho lives in personal autonomy. Adults and children are valued for their sheer being, just because they *are*. There is no urge toward achievement; no one has to strive for success. In fact, neither is there reward for success, nor is success held out as a reward for hard work. Wealth may be the result of hard work and skill, but obviously it is also the blatant result of lack of generosity, lack of responsibility for one's relatives, perhaps even of malicious witchcraft. No good Navaho becomes and remains 'wealthy' in our terms. . . .

"This attitude is basic to all Navaho relatedness, so that here man is not burdened with guilt and does not feel apologetic toward human or divine beings. He is neither grateful nor abject to his gods, and, as a matter of fact, he must never humble himself before them, since the process of healing, of the recovery of harmony with the universe, involves identification with the appropriate god, who would be slighted if the patient humiliates himself. This means that the Navaho has— and indeed must have—as much respect and value for himself as for others; in fact, this is the Navaho version of the principle that we have discovered so recently in our society: that we cannot accept and respect others until we learn to accept and respect ourselves. . . .

"So the individual remains inviolate. No one coerces another among the Navaho. Parents do not force their children to do what they un- equivocally do not want to do, such as going to school or to the hospital; children are not coerced even 'for their own good.' As the mother of two unschooled children put it, 'I listen to my children, and I have to take their word.' There is no political coercion, and all leadership is traditionally incidental. A man finds himself in a position of leadership when the people seek him out because of the high degree of his inner development; because of his wisdom, his knowledge, his assumption of responsibility, his physical skill and hardihood, the wealth which he is always ready to use to help his relatives. Men do not seek leadership; and White employers have found that the Navaho are reluctant to become foremen, however able they may be, and in spite of the higher pay involved. It is 'fundamentally indecent,' according to Clyde Kluckhohn, 'for a single individual to presume to make decisions for the group,' and therefore not even a leader will make decisions for others, or give orders to others. . . .

"The practices I have presented here are not for us to copy, but rather food for thought, the basis for new insights. I have tried to show that law and limits and personal autonomy can coexist effectively, that spontaneity is not necessarily killed by group responsibility, that respect for individual integrity is not an end to be achieved by specific means, but that it can exist only if it is supported by deep conviction and by the entire way of life." ("Individual Autonomy and Social Structure," by Dorothy Lee; *The Personal Guidance Journal,* September 1956.)

Here is another anthropologist, Clyde Kluckhohn, saying pretty much the same thing about us contemporary Americans (in *The American Style: Essays in Value and Performance,* Harper Brothers, 1958).

Kluckhohn starts by quoting Tocqueville, who is as habit-forming for social scientists as the *Federalist* is for learned lawyers. Here is Tocqueville:

"I know of no country in which there is so little independence of mind and real freedom of discussion as in America. The will of man is not shattered, but softened, bent, and guided; men are seldom forced by it to act, but they are constantly restrained from acting. Such a power does not destroy, but it prevents existence; it does not tyrannize, but it compresses, enervates, extinguishes, and stupefies a people.

. . . The majority no longer says: 'You shall think as I do or you shall die'; but it says: 'You are free to think differently from me and to retain your life, your property, and all that you possess; but you are henceforth a stranger among your people. You may retain your civil rights, but they will be useless to you, for you will never be chosen by your fellow citizens if you solicit their votes; and they will affect to scorn you if you ask for their esteem.

" 'You will remain among men, but you will be deprived of the rights of mankind. Your fellow creatures will shun you like an impure being; and even those who believe in your innocence will abandon you, lest they should be shunned in their turn. Go in peace! I have given you your life, but there is an existence worse than death.' "

And now Kluckhohn:

"It is true that American official standards have always been better described in terms of 'public approval' than as either 'materialistic' or 'idealistic.' There is also considerable truth in the saying that 'standardization is the primal crime of democracy.' Yet it is ridiculous to accept literally the statements of some superficial European observers about 'the dreary uniformity of American life.' We must only grant with Perry that while Americans do not easily accept authority from above, they have ever been 'highly vulnerable to the impersonal and unorganized authority of their social environment.' . . .

"Today's kind of 'conformity' may actually be a step toward more genuine individuality in the United States. 'Conformity' is less of a personal and psychological problem—less tinged with anxiety and guilt. I have a hunch—from reading some of the literature on Puritanism in both its New England and frontier forms—that the only way the American Puritan could lower his guilt level was by participating in a group—especially (but not exclusively) a religious group. To the extent that the Puritan Ethic has declined one would therefore expect that the whole problem of conformity was less compulsive and emotional in both its affirmative and negative directions. If one accepts outwardly the conventions of one's group, one may have greater psychic energy to develop and fulfill one's private potentialities as a unique person. I have encountered no substantial evidence that this 'conformity' is thoroughgoingly 'inward.' Nor am I convinced that even in the 'McCarthy period' more than a tiny minority of Americans spelled loyalty: c-o-n-f-o-r-m-i-t-y. . . .

"At any rate I am convinced that much of the contemporary 'conformity' springs from deliberate and somewhat reflective choice based both upon realization of the uncertainty of things and upon recognition of the implacable necessities of gigantic organizations. Possibly 'conformity' may also be a reaction to exhaustion brought about by the speed and number of changes. . . .

"However much 'conformity' may have increased, no one can argue that attention to the psyche of the individual has dropped out of the picture. On the contrary, concern with 'mental health,' with the proper psychological atmosphere at home and in the school, with psychotherapy, has risen to proportions that some have, understandably, regarded as obsessive. This has been associated with the domestication of psychoanalysis on the American scene and the immense increase in psychological self-consciousness in mass dimensions.

"Little review is required, for the phenomena face us daily in conversation, in the movies, in almost every book or periodical we read. I shall only run through a few illustrations by way of reminder. Aldredge speaks of the 'preoccupation with . . . psychological *problems*' in the novels of the forties and in the novels of the fifties of 'signs of concentration upon rather thin childhood and domestic situations in which the drama tends to center in a subtle psychic conflict between characters. . . .' Sutton *et al* comment that: 'To a remarkable degree, children are now raised according to what are currently conceived to be sound psychological principles rather than according to traditional moral norms.'

"Strunsky writes of 'the cult of personality' in political life. Inkeles shows that Americans (both those with a college education and those with only a secondary education) attribute national characteristics to child-rearing and psychological factors more (by a considerable margin) than do samples from eight European countries and from Mexico.

"Mead makes some perceptive observations:

" '. . . what increase in self-consciousness can be invoked to explain the present trend which so revolts our systematically and recurrently revolted critics of the American scene? . . . This increase in self-conscious reflexive response to partly accurate, partly contrived pictures of what young executives, career girls, Americans overseas or exurbanites do, think, say, feel, what they read, eat, wear, and believe, may indeed have lamentable consequences, although they are not the consequences that are immediately prophesied by the critics. It may also be suggested that this reflective state in which we live is a kind of stepchild of some of the most important developments of the last quarter century—of increased awareness of ourselves as individuals with a partly forgotten past, as members of a culture many of whose values are unformulated but nonetheless real. It would be easy to blame our present state on an exaggerated self-consciousness which has destroyed both innocence and spontaneity. But it may also be blamed upon those who have used the tools which have been developed by the therapist, the teacher and the research scholar as implements of manipulation within a system which they despised and hated, often quite unfairly, but from which they continued to draw a livelihood. The frustrated novelist who sells his soul to an advertising agency or a public relations firm, the frustrated liberal who condones the use of sensational sex stories to sell a politically liberal newspaper, the cynical reformer who thinks the only way to get members of Congress to do a good deed is to offer them bad rationalizations—these are among the people who, out of disillusion, self-contempt, and contempt for their employers and their audiences, have helped to construct this world of semi-truths and manipulated backgrounds and faked shadows within which young people find the images on which to model their lives—and so seem to their elders to be "conforming." ' . . .

"*Heterogeneity as a value.* Heterogeneity is itself becoming one of the organizing principles of American culture. This tendency has two origins. One goes back to the realization of the bewildering rapidity of change and is reflected in an implicit premise of much American life and especially American education: you never can tell what strange oddment of information will be interesting or indeed useful in an unforeseen context. Americans are devoted to newspaper columns and drawings of the 'Believe It or Not' type and to TV programs of the '$64,000 Question' variety. Americans, perhaps, are following a way of thinking suited to a world in which generalizations are hard to apply.

"The other origin lies in increased experience with cultural diversity and a diminished certainty about the infallible superiority of 'the American way of life' in every last idea and detail. One of the massive facts of the last twenty years is the vast jump in the number of Americans who have actually seen other cultures. Twenty million have served in the armed forces, and a high proportion of these have been abroad. It would be naïve to assume that a majority of these have been much affected one way or the other (one small study—Smith, 1945—indicates the effects are not great), and we all know from personal observation that sometimes the effects are negative. Nevertheless, some are enlightened and the consequences of this in the body politic gradually become cumulative. It is difficult in the military setting to have other than somewhat artificial and superficial experiences, though a surprising number of individuals manage to do so. Americans traveling in foreign countries since 1945 for pleasure and as civilian representatives of government or business have better opportunities, and the American masses are far less hermetically isolated from first-hand or one-remove contact with 'foreign ways'—other than those of immigrants who were traditionally looked down upon and were, for the most part, not representative of the 'higher' levels of their cultures. Finally, there is the circumstance that all fairly well-informed Americans, even if themselves untraveled, are aware—however grudgingly— that the realities of international politics will not permit the writing off of other values and customs as simply 'ignorant' or 'stupid.' . . .

"One must not, of course, be too cheerful. Erikson warns that the tolerant appraisal of other identities endangers one's own. And not all soberly factual opinion agrees to the increase in acceptance of diversity. One of the investigations in greatest depth (Adorno et al., 1950) finds little spontaneity but much compulsiveness, whether this shows itself in apathy, surface piety or active racism. They conclude that those Americans who are relatively free of ethnocentrism tend to be neurotic and indecisive. These authors believe the sado-masochistic type is growing in numbers because of a steady increase in monopolistic domination of American life. Likewise, they see the mass media as leading to increased confusion, cynicism, and conformity on the parts of Americans.

"Having reviewed the evidence, however, I would put my money on Stouffer's appraisal:

" 'Great social, economic, and technological forces are operating slowly and imperceptibly on the side of spreading tolerance. The rising level of education and the accompanying decline in authoritarian child-rearing practices increase independence of thought and respect for others whose ideas are different. The increasing geographical movement of people has a similar consequence, as well as the vicarious experiences supplied by the magic of our ever more powerful media of communication.' "

If security is the chassis, anxiety may be the ignition. Margaret Mead will give you pause:

"When critics wish to repudiate the world in which we live today, one of their familiar ways of doing it is to castigate modern man because anxiety is his chief problem. This they say, in W. H. Auden's phrase, is the age of anxiety. This is what we have arrived at with all our vaunted progress, our great technological advances, our great wealth—everyone goes about with a burden of anxiety so enormous that, in the end, our stomachs and our arteries and our skins express the tension under which we live. Americans who have lived in Europe come back to comment on our favorite farewell which, instead of the old goodbye (God be with you), is now 'Take it easy,' each American admonishing the other not to break down from the tension and strain of modern life.

"Whenever an age is characterized by a phrase, it is presumably in contrast to other ages. If we are the age of anxiety, what were other ages? And here the critics and carpers do a very amusing thing. First, they give us lists of the opposites of anxiety: security, trust, self-confidence, self-direction. Then, without much further discussion, they let us assume that other ages, other periods of history, were somehow the ages of trust or confident direction.

"The savage who, on his South Sea island, simply sat and let bread fruit fall into his lap, the simple peasant, at one with the fields he ploughed and the beasts he tended, the craftsman busy with his tools and lost in the fulfillment of the instinct of workmanship—these are the counter-images conjured up by descriptions of the strain under which men live today. But no one who lived in those days has returned to testify how paradisiacal they really were.

"Certainly if we observe and question the savages or simple peasants in the world today, we find something quite different. The untouched savage in the middle of New Guinea isn't anxious; he is seriously and continually *frightened*—of black magic, of enemies with spears who may kill him or his wives and children at any moment, while they stoop to drink from a spring, or climb a palm tree for a coconut. He goes warily, day and night, taut and fearful.

"As for the peasant populations of a great part of the world, they aren't so much anxious as hungry. They aren't anxious about whether they will get a salary raise, or which of the three colleges of their choice they will be admitted to, or whether to buy a Ford or Cadillac, or whether the kind of TV set they want is too expensive. They are hungry, cold and, in many parts of the world, they dread that local warfare, bandits, political coups, may endanger their homes, their meager livelihoods and their lives. But surely they are not anxious.

"For anxiety, as we have come to use it to describe our characteristic state of mind, can be contrasted with the active fear of hunger, loss, violence and death. Anxiety is the appropriate emotion when the immediate personal terror—of a volcano, an arrow, the sorcerer's spell, a stab in the back and other calamities, all directed against one's self—disappears. . . .

"On balance, our age of anxiety represents a large advance over savage and peasant cultures. Out of a productive system of technology drawing upon enormous resources, we have created a nation in which anxiety has replaced terror and despair, for all except the severely disturbed. The specter of hunger means something only to those Americans who can identify themselves with the millions of hungry people on other continents. The specter of terror may still be roused in some by a knock at the door in a few parts of the South, or in those who have just escaped from a totalitarian regime or who have kin still behind the Curtains.

"But in this twilight world which is neither at peace nor at war, and where there is insurance against certain immediate, downright, personal disasters, for most Americans there remains only anxiety over what may happen, might happen, could happen.

"This is the world out of which grows the hope, for the first time in history, of a society where there will be freedom from want and freedom from fear. Our very anxiety is born of our knowledge of what is now possible for each and for all. The number of people who consult psychiatrists today is not, as is sometimes felt, a symptom of increasing mental ill health, but rather the precursor of a world in which the hope of genuine mental health will be open to everyone, a world in which no individual feels that he need be hopelessly brokenhearted, a failure, a menace to others or a traitor to himself. . . .

"Worry in an empty context means that men die daily little deaths. But good anxiety—not about the things that were left undone long ago, that return to haunt and harry men's minds, but active, vivid anxiety about what must be done and that quickly—binds men to life with an intense concern.

"This is still a world in which too many of the wrong things happen somewhere. But this is a world in which we now have the means to make a great many more of the right things happen everywhere. For Americans, the generalization which a Swedish social scientist made about our attitudes on race relations is true in many other fields: anticipated change which we feel is right and necessary but difficult makes us unduly anxious and apprehensive, but such change, once consummated, brings a glow of relief. We are still a people who—in the literal sense—believe in making good." (From *The New York Times* Magazine Section, May 20, 1956.)

Immanence, symbolism, patterns, and folkways. The only other avenue of approach to an understanding that I know of goes through the gates of language; and all I can do is show you the gate. Anyone who opens up the subject of language engages in something only a little less large than life. Here is a toe in the door.

Clyde Kluckhohn puts it neatly. In his book on the Navahos, with Dorothea Leighton (Harvard University Press, 1947), there are these two paragraphs:

"Any language is more than an instrument for the conveying of ideas, more even than an instrument for working upon the feelings of others and for self-expression. Every language is also a means of categorizing experience. What people think and feel, is determined, to be sure, by their individual physiological state, by their personal history, and by what actually happens in the outside world. But it is also determined by a factor which is often overlooked—namely, the pattern of linguistic habits which people have acquired as members of a particular society. The events of the 'real' world are never felt or reported as a machine would do it. There is a selection process and an interpretation in the very act of response. Some features of the external situation are highlighted; others are ignored or not fully discriminated.

"Every people has its own characteristic classes in which individuals pigeonhole their experience. These classes are established primarily by the language through the types of objects, processes, or qualities which receive special emphasis in the vocabulary and equally, though more subtly, through the types of differentiation or activity which are distinguished in grammatical forms. The language says, as it were, 'Notice this,' 'Always consider this separate from that,' 'Such-and-such things belong together.' Since persons are trained from infancy to respond in these ways they take such discriminations for granted, as part of the inescapable stuff of life. But when we see two peoples with different social traditions respond in different ways to what appear to the outsider to be identical stimulus-situations, we realize that experience is much less a 'given,' an absolute, than we thought. Every language has an effect upon what the people who use it see, what they feel, how they think, what they can talk about."

Stephen Ullmann puts it this way (*Words and Their Use,* Philosophical Library, 1951) :

"We have come to regard the vocabulary as a kind of framework, a ready-made system of classification, which we inherit from our ancestors and which shapes and fashions our own vision of the universe. It is the depository of the work of many generations, a vehicle of traditional values, beliefs, and modes of interpretation. Every speech-community evolves its own unique way of linguistic expression, in which its whole outlook and philosophy of life are enshrined. To be born into the speech-community is to inherit the mode of vision and the scale of values peculiar to it and crystallized in its language."

They tell me that this is the Sapir-Whorf hypothesis. Let us go to the sources. A paragraph from Sapir (*Science*, Volume 74, p. 578) and another from Whorf (*Collected Papers on Metalinguistics*, Department of State, Washington, 1952) will serve as an introduction. So far as I know, no one else has gone any further, except to raise doubts and queries, which you can do as well as another. I take two quotations from *Language in Culture* (University of Chicago Press, 1954).

Sapir says, "Language is not merely a more or less systematic inventory of the various items of experience which seem relevant to the individual, as is so often naïvely assumed, but is also a self-contained, creative symbolic organization, which not only refers to experience largely acquired without its help but actually defines experience for us by reason of its formal completeness and because of our unconscious projection of its implicit expectations into the field of experience. In this respect language is very much like a mathematical system which, also, records experience in the truest sense of the word, only in its crudest beginnings, but, as time goes on, becomes elaborated into a self-contained conceptual system which previsages all possible experience in accordance with certain accepted formal limitations. Meanings are not so much discovered in experience as imposed upon it, because of the tyrannical hold that linguistic form has upon our orientation in the world."

Whorf says that "the linguistic system (in other words, the grammar) of each language is not merely a reproducing instrument for voicing ideas but rather is itself the shaper of ideas, the program and guide for the individual's mental activity, for his analysis of impressions, for his synthesis of his mental stock in trade. . . . We dissect nature along lines laid down by our native languages. The categories and types that we isolate from the world of phenomena we do not find there because they stare every observer in the face; on the contrary, the world is presented in a kaleidoscopic flux of impressions which has to be organized by our minds—and this means largely by the linguistic systems in our minds."

Supplementary to page 12.

It's a far cry, but the other day I was struck by a likeness between the way the Court went about construing one of these large terms with so little meaning of their own, these merely directional words like "due process," "equal protection," and so on, with the way Paul Valéry said he expected his readers and critics to enjoy his verse.

I wonder if it is too far to be heard. I don't think it is. I don't believe it is any farther than the distance between any two aesthetic values or satisfactions. Whitehead remarked, you will recall, that the Court gives its decisions "on the basis of the aesthetic satisfaction" it gets from harmonizing the Constitution with modern America. May not this satisfaction be similar to the satisfaction that an attentive reader takes in extracting a meaning from a difficult poem?

Here's what Valéry said. I take it from Denise Folliot's translation of the preface Valéry wrote for Alain's comments on Valéry's volume of verse, Charmes (Valéry, The Art of Poetry, Pantheon Books, 1958; pp. 155 ff.).

"My verses have the meaning attributed to them. The one I give them suits only myself and does not contradict anyone else. It is an error contrary to the nature of poetry, and one which may even be fatal to it, to claim that for each poem there is a corresponding true meaning, unique and conformable to, or identical with, some thought of the author's. . . .

"There is no question in poetry of transmitting to one person something intelligible happening within another. It is a question of creating within the former a state whose expression is exactly and peculiarly what communicates it to him. Whatever image or emotion is formed in the lover of poetry has value and sufficiency if it produces in him this reciprocal relation between cause-word and effect-word. As a result, such a reader enjoys very great freedom as to ideas, a freedom analogous to that which music allows to the hearer, although less extensive.

"Once a work is finished and presented, whether in verse or prose, its author can propose or affirm nothing about it that would have any more weight or would explain it more exactly than what anyone else might say. A work is an object or event of the senses, whereas the various values or interpretations it suggests are consequences (ideas or affections) which cannot alter it in its entirely material capacity to produce quite different ones. . . . An author can, no doubt, inform us of his intentions; but it is not a question of these; it is a question of what subsists, what he has made independent of himself. . . .

"There exist certain rather mysterious bodies which are studied in physics and used in chemistry; I always think of them when considering works of art. The simple presence of these bodies in a particular mixture of other substances determines the latter to unite, the former remaining unaltered, identical with themselves, neither transformed in their nature nor increased or diminished in their quantity. They are then, present and absent, acting and not acted upon. Such is the text of a work. The action of its presence modifies minds, each according to its nature and state, provoking combinations latent within a certain head, but whatever reaction is thus produced, the text is found to be unaltered and capable of indefinitely generating other phenomena in other circumstances or in another person."

We are talking about the Constitution. You don't have to agree with Valéry about poetry. Edmund Wilson doesn't agree at all. He thinks this is "an excessively esoteric conception of poetry." In his *Axel's Castle* (Scribner, 1931), Wilson says:

"This conception is most clearly stated and its weakness, it seems to me, made most clearly manifest in a preface which Valéry has just contributed to a commentary on his own *Charmes* by the French essayist Alain (this scholastic layer upon layer of commentary is itself very characteristic of the contemporary criticism of poetry). Here we find, as usual, the scientific approach—which it occurs to us, as we read, is largely a matter of scientific similes: 'There are certain rather mysterious bodies which physics studies and which chemistry uses: I always think of them when I reflect upon works of art.' These are the catalytic agents, which precipitate chemical changes without being affected themselves. So the work of art, says Valéry, acts upon the mind into which it is introduced. Even when chemically considered, then, the work of art remains something 'mysterious.' And by 'works of art,' it further appears that, in the department of literature, Valéry means poetry exclusively. Prose, he says, has 'sense' for its sole object—but the object of poetry is something not only more mysterious but also apparently more occult: 'There is absolutely no question in poetry of one person's transmitting to another something intelligible that is going on in his mind. It is a question of creating in the latter a state whose expression is precisely and uniquely that which communicates it to him. Whatever image or emotion is formed in the amateur of poems, it is valid and sufficient if it produces in him this reciprocal relation between the word-cause and the word-effect. The result is that the reader enjoys a very great freedom in regard to ideas, a freedom analogous to that which one recognizes in the case of the hearer of music, though not so intensive.'

"It seems to me that a pretense to exactitude is here used to cover a number of ridiculously false assumptions, and to promote a kind of aesthetic mysticism rather than to effect a scientific analysis. In the first place, is it not absurd to assert that prose deals exclusively in 'sense' as distinguished from suggestion, and that one has no right to expect from poetry, as Valéry says in another passage, 'any definite notion at all'? Is verse really an intellectual product absolutely different in kind from prose? Has it really an absolutely different function? Are not both prose and verse, after all, merely techniques of human intercommunication, and techniques which have played various roles, have been used for various purposes, in different periods and civilizations? The early Greeks used verse for their histories, their romances, and their laws—the Greeks and the Elizabethans used it for their dramas. If Valéry's definitions are correct, what becomes of Homer, Virgil, Dante, Shakespeare, and Goethe? They all of them deal in sense as well as suggestion and aim to convey 'definite notions.' "

I offer you another paragraph from Valéry, because it seems to me unmistakably to apply to both poetry and the Constitution. It is in Valéry's preface to Gustave Cohen's essay on Valéry's *Le Cimetière Marin*. Again in Denise Folliot's translation (p. 152):

"As for the interpretation of the *letter*, I have already made myself clear elsewhere on this point; but it can never be too much insisted upon: *there is no true meaning to a text*—no author's authority. Whatever he may have *wanted to say*, he has written what he has written. Once published, a text is like an apparatus that anyone may use as he will and according to his ability: it is not certain that the one who constructed it can use it better than another. Besides, if he knows well what he meant to do, this knowledge always disturbs his perception of what he has done."

I heartily agree, and I have said as much myself a number of times in *It's Your Law* (Harvard University Press, 1954; pp. 44-81) and in an article, "A Better Theory of Legal Interpretation," in *Jurisprudence in Action* (Association of the Bar of the City of New York, 1953).

Just the same, I share André Gide's feelings when I read Valéry.

Gide said in his *Journal* (on July 17, 1941), *"A lire Valéry on ac-
quiert cette sagesse de se sentir un peu plus sot qu'avant."*

&

The distinction between coercion and persuasion runs into theology.
Whitehead comments, in his *Adventures of Ideas,* on "Plato's final
conviction towards the end of his life, that the divine element in the
world is to be conceived as a persuasive agency and not as a coercive
agency. This doctrine should be looked upon as one of the greatest
intellectual discoveries in the history of religion. It is plainly enunci-
ated by Plato, though he failed to co-ordinate it systematically with
the rest of his metaphysical theory. Indeed, Plato always failed in his
attempts at systematization, and always succeeded in displaying depth
of metaphysical intuition—the greatest metaphysician, the poorest
systematic thinker.

"The alternative doctrine, prevalent then and now, sees either
in the many gods or in the one God the final coercive forces
wielding the thunder. By a metaphysical sublimation of this
doctrine of God as the supreme agency of compulsion, he is transformed into the one supreme reality, omnipotently disposing a wholly
derivative world. Plato wavered inconsistently between these diverse
conceptions. But he does finally enunciate without qualification the
doctrine of the divine persuasion, by reason of which ideals are effective in the world and forms of order evolve."

&* *Supplementary to page 15.*

There is more than this to the *Antigone.* E. M. Forster, after admit-
ting that he did not suppose he could have written the *Divine Comedy*

or Gibbon's *Decline and Fall of the Roman Empire,* says, "I don't even think I could have written the *Antigone* of Sophocles, though of all the great tragic utterances that comes closest to my heart, that is my central faith." (*Two Cheers for Democracy,* Harcourt, Brace; p. 222.)

Forster is thinking of Antigone herself, just as Walter Kaufmann is when he says, "People think of *Antigone* as a play, if at all; and a few know that line which defies adequate translation into English: 'Not to hate with those who hate, but to love with those who love, I live.' The modern reader finds Antigone almost Christian. But what great Christian ever defied his age instead of making concessions to it and sharing its prejudices to the point of reinforcing and sanctifying them? What great Christian did what he considered right, like Antigone, without hope of any reward whatever, and without any vengefulness toward those he defied?

"Traditional Judaism was a religion by which one could live and for which one could die. Early Christianity was a religion by which one could not live, but for which one could die. By Buddhism one can live, though one cannot die for it. But by what is today called religion one cannot live, nor could one die for it. How much more profound is the outlook of the great tragic poets! What is there to prevent a man from living and dying like Antigone?

"What we find in Sophocles is an outlook which will probably never be understood by many. But the vast majority who do not understand him are likely to have a very limited notion of religion, too." (*Critique of Religion and Philosophy,* Harper, 1958; p. 245.)

ᕈ Supplementary to page 20

I cannot absolutely deny determinism. No one could do that, or want to, after reading this by Isaiah Berlin:

"For it is plainly a good thing that we should be reminded by social scientists that the scope of human choice is a good deal more limited than we used to suppose; that the evidence at our disposal shows that many of the acts too often assumed to be within the individual's control are not so; that man is an object in nature to a larger degree than has at times been supposed, that human beings more often than not act as they do because of characteristics due to heredity or physical or social environment or education, or biological laws or physical characteristics or the interplay of these factors with each other, and with the obscurer factors loosely called psychical characteristics; and that the resultant habits of thought, feeling, and expression are as capable of being classified and made subject to hypotheses and systematic prediction as the behavior of material objects. And this certainly alters our ideas about the limits of freedom and responsibility. If we are told that a given case of stealing is due to kleptomania, we protest that the appropriate treatment is not punishment but a remedy for a disease; and similarly, if a destructive act of a vicious character is ascribed to a specific psychological or social cause, we decide, if we are convinced that the explanation is valid, that the agent is not responsible for his acts and consequently deserves therapeutic rather than penal treatment. It is salutary to be reminded of the narrowness of the field within which we can begin to claim to be free; and some would claim that such knowledge is still increasing, and the field still contracting. Where the frontier between freedom and causal laws is to be determined is a crucial practical issue; knowledge of it is a powerful and indispensable antidote to ignorance and irrationality, and offers us new types of explanation—historical, psychological, sociological, biological—which previous generations have lacked. What we cannot alter, or can alter less than we had supposed, can hardly be used as evidence for or against us as free moral agents; it can cause us to feel pride, shame, regret, interest, but not remorse; it can be admired, envied, deplored, enjoyed, feared, wondered at, but not praised or condemned; our tendency to indignation is curbed, we desist from passing judgment. . . .

"Social determinism is, at least historically, closely bound up with the ideals of sociology. And it may, indeed, be a true doctrine. But if it is true, and if we begin to take it seriously, then, indeed, the changes in our language, our moral notions, our attitudes toward one another, our views of history, of society and of everything else will be too profound to be even adumbrated. The concepts of praise and blame, innocence and guilt, and individual responsibility, from which we started, are but a small element in the structure, which would collapse or disappear. If social and psychological determinism were established as an accepted truth, our world would be transformed far more radically than was the teleological world of the classical and middle ages by the triumphs of mechanistic principles or those of natural selection. Our words—our modes of speech and thought— would be transformed in literally unimaginable ways; the notions of choice, of voluntary action, of responsibility, freedom, are so deeply embedded in our outlook that our new life, as creatures in a world genuinely lacking these concepts, can, I should maintain, literally not be conceived by us. But there is, as yet, no need to alarm ourselves unduly. We are speaking only of pseudoscientific ideals; the reality is not in sight. The evidence for a thoroughgoing determinism is not to hand; and if there is a persistent tendency to believe in it in some theoretical fashion, that is surely due far more to a 'scientistic' or metaphysical ideal, or to a longing to lay down moral burdens, or minimize individual responsibility and transfer it to impersonal forces which can be safely accused of causing all our discontents, than to any increase in our powers of critical reflection or any improvement in our scientific techniques. Belief in historical determinism of this type is, of course, very widespread, particularly in its Marxist, its psychological, and its sociological forms; and in what I should like to call its 'historiosophical' form too, by which I mean metaphysico-theological theories of history, which attract many who have lost their faith in older religious orthodoxies." (*Historical Inevitability*, by Isaiah Berlin, Oxford University Press, 1954; p. 35-36; 75-76.)

🙖 *Supplementary to page 21ff.*

On page 21 of the text, I try to show why lawyers resist the idea of an absolute. They are on firm philosophical ground. Witness A. J. Ayer:

"There must be absolute values, it is said, for otherwise there would be no reason for our preferring one course of conduct to another, for approving or condemning anything whatsoever. And there must be a God, for otherwise no values could be absolute. I think it is worth taking a little time to show that both steps in this argument are altogether invalid.

"To begin with the second. It could be the case that belief in the existence of a God was causally necessary to make people behave in ways that were conventionally considered to be right. I take this indeed to be the point of Voltaire's dictum that if God did not exist it would be necessary to invent him; it is the somewhat cynical suggestion that the mass of people can be induced to submit to conventional morality only by the fear of future punishment or the hope of future reward. I doubt very much myself whether this is true, but it is a matter for sociological investigation. One would have to see whether there was a positive correlation between the fidelity shown by the members of a specimen community to its moral standards and the prevalence among them of religious belief: and, assuming that there were such a correlation, whether or not it was accidental. But, whatever the result of such an investigation, it would have no bearing at all upon the thesis that the maintenance of values, whether absolute or not, *logically* requires the existence of God. For to see that this thesis is false we need only consider what Leibnitz, himself a theist, long ago pointed out: that unless one's judgments of value were logically independent of the attribution of any properties to God, the claim that God is good, which is fundamental to the view we are discussing, would itself be without significance. So long as we have some independent criterion for deciding what is good, then those who believe in God, and believe that he is good, may reasonably be grateful that he satisfies it. But if all that were meant by saying of something that it was good was that it was willed by God, then his goodness would be nothing to be grateful for. For to say that he willed only what was good, would then be to express the mere tautology that he willed what he willed. However diabolical his behavior, it would still by definition be good. That God is good, or that he wills only what is good, may be, for those who can believe in him, a reason, that is to say a motive, for doing what they think they ought: but it cannot be the *ground* for the goodness or badness of what they do. Consequently, even if there were absolute values, their existence would not have the slightest tendency to prove, or indeed to disprove, the existence of God. The two questions are quite independent, and there is no warrant for confusing them." (*Philosophy at Absolute Zero*, by A. J. Ayer, in *Encounter*, London, October 1955.)

Holmes's "poor devil who has no other way of reaching the superlative" except by getting drunk is treated more respectfully by William James, whom I cite on page 21 of the text as having said that intoxication makes a man "one with the cosmos." It is sometimes imprudent to check your quotations. I find that James actually wrote that drunkenness makes a man "for the moment one with truth." Here is the whole paragraph, from his *The Varieties of Religious Experience*:

"The next step into mystical states carries us into a realm that public opinion and ethical philosophy have long since branded as pathological, though private practice and certain lyric strains of poetry seem still to bear witness to its ideality. I refer to the consciousness produced by intoxicants and anesthetics, especially by alcohol. The sway of alcohol over mankind is unquestionably due to its power to stimulate the mystical faculties of human nature, usually crushed to earth by the cold facts and dry criticisms of the sober hour. Sobriety diminishes, discriminates, and says no; drunkenness expands, unites, and says yes. It is in fact the great exciter of the *Yes* function in man. It brings its votary from the chill periphery of things to the radiant core. It makes him for the moment one with truth. Not through mere perversity do men run after it. To the poor and the unlettered it stands in the place of symphony concerts and of literature; and it is part of the deeper mystery and tragedy of life that whiffs and gleams of something that we immediately recognize as excellent should be vouchsafed to so many of us only in the fleeting earlier phases of what in its totality is so degrading a poisoning. The drunken consciousness is one bit of the mystic consciousness, and our total opinion of it must find its place in our opinion of that larger whole." (Pp. 386-7)

❧ *Supplementary to page 26.*

Here is the passage from Learned Hand that inspired my final paragraph on page 26 about the Absolute. Hand is speaking to lawyers at the opening of a Conference on the Continuing Education of the Bar at Arden House on December 16, 1958:

"Remember what Justice Holmes said about 'Justice.' I don't know what you think about him but on the whole he was to me the master craftsman certainly of our time; and he said, 'I hate justice,' which he didn't quite mean. What he did mean was this. I remember once I was with him; it was a Saturday when the court was to confer. It was before he had a motorcar; and we jogged along in an old coupé. When we got down to the Capitol, I wanted to provoke a response, so as he walked off, I said to him, 'Well, sir, goodbye. Do justice!' He turned quite sharply and he said, 'Come here. Come here.' I answered, 'Oh, I know, I know.' He replied, 'That is not my job. My job is to play the game according to the rules.' I have never forgotten that. I have tried to follow, though oftentimes I found that I didn't know what the rules were. Ulpian, as you remember, said that justice is to insure to 'each one his own.' Well, what is 'his own'? How are you going to tell what 'his own' is? Does anybody know? As they say in English, 'My submission, my Lord, is that you can't measure values.' Values are incommensurables. You can get a solution only by a compromise, or call it what you will. It must be one that people won't complain of too much; but you cannot expect any more objective measure.

"That is not the fault of law. Often we do think of law as though it was unique in its uncertainty; but that is not so. I was greatly interested recently to learn that there is the same infirmity in other branches of human activity, even in the case of physics, which we think is of all disciplines the most likely to have quantitative and absolute determinations. I don't profess to be able to understand what I read; but the results in physics are apparently very shifty. They are as shifty as we are as to what they really mean. I remember reading something of Oppenheimer's, one of the big shots, you might say. He was talking about the new elements that entered into the nucleus of the atom. They keep growing in number more and more, more and more. I was entertained by the names that they keep coining. Better still, there is a story, though it may not be true, for I don't remember where I got it. It was about Niels Bohr, who is a great fellow in physics. He was the one who determined that an atom was a planetary system. You had the proton and the electrons going around at unimaginable velocities. That seemed awfully good; but now no one believes in that kind of atom. Then Heisenberg, another great man, comes along and says, 'There ain't no rules in this game. An electron may make up its mind to go backward or any other way. It is all a question of statistics.' God forbid that I should suppose that I understand how you can have statistics that mean anything when you have no initial constant bias; but the story is that a lot of these great men—perhaps almost as great as those here—were talking. Heisenberg got off something new, and Niels Bohr—who, in spite of the fact of the disruption of his planetary system, still ranks 'tops'—said to him, 'Heisenberg, what you say is just nonsense. There is no sense in it. It begins and it ends, and there ain't anything. But I don't know; fifty years from now, maybe everybody will be agreeing with what you say.'

"I sometimes feel a good deal like that when I hear about the eternal principles of jurisprudence; 'That is what you say now, but fifty years from now no one will believe it.' Of course you have got to have in your society some at least provisional but authoritative compromises, some tentative solution. When I say 'authoritative,' I mean those that have sanctions. What shall these adjustments be? You can take your pick. If you can find any general principles that are concrete enough to serve as guides, that do not contain question-begging adjectives or nouns, and that really show that you are saying anything, I should like to have you show them to me. I don't know them.

"The most that you can ask, I think, is that they shall be most likely to secure assent and not provoke resistance. How far ahead are you to look? I don't know. All I can say is that I mean by law those adjustments which will be most likely to be accepted for a period that you needn't now look beyond; and when you go beyond that period, then I say what Niels Bohr said to Heisenberg.

"What are the qualities which give any measure of hope that you will succeed in what you are here undertaking if you should proceed in that way? What is the temper, whether you are on the Bench or at the Bar or in a legislature, which is most likely to result in that kind of generalization? First, it seems to me, is imagination. You must be able successfully to realize how other people in the society with which you are concerned are likely to respond to the adjustments that you propose; how far will it be necessary to enforce compliance? How far will the people accept it as, on the whole, the best they can get for the time being? Of course, you must have impartiality. What do I mean by impartiality? I mean you mustn't introduce yourself, your own preconceived notions about what is right. You must try, so far as you can—it's impossible for human beings to do it absolutely— but just so far as you can, not to interject your own personal interests, even your own preconceived assumptions and beliefs. And (this is one of the things that we most often forget) you must have enough courage to back up what you know to be provisional conclusions which tomorrow may show to be untrue.

"The combination of these qualities is one of the hardest achievements; but it is, I submit, the essence of adult education. If we lawyers really learn our job we must acquire this temper, this disposition, this attitude—call it what you like, though it is one of the rarest accomplishments of human beings.

"Moreover, advocacy is its enemy, as is very well put in the report of your Joint Conference. But we are not merely advocates, and we must not always be advocates. Adult education means that we have got rid of inveterate advocacy, except in so far as we may advocate what we are disinterested in, if that be possible. I wonder whether the best mood or habit is not that, forgetting for the time our job as lawyers, we should think of human beings as a whole, we should look at life *sub specie aeternitatis* and yet believe that all specific choices may be momentous. And how can we do that unless we reserve to ourselves substantial periods and intervals when we can withdraw and reflect in detachment?

"So, you will excuse me if, as I thought about what I should say to you, there came to me (you may think this is absurd, and I give it as a personal confession) that very great sonnet of Wordsworth's that you know, as the approach, the feeling (I don't know how else to put it), that is, I think, particularly appropriate to us:

> The world is too much with us; late and soon,
> Getting and spending, we lay waste our powers:
> Little we see in Nature that is ours.
> We have given our hearts away, a sordid boon.
> The sea that bares her bosom to the moon,
> The winds that will be howling at all hours
> And are upgathered now like sleeping flowers,
> For this, for everything, we are out of tune.
> It moves us not.
>   Great God, I'd rather be
> A Pagan, suckled in a creed outworn,
> So might I, standing on this pleasant lea,
> Have glimpses that would make me less forlorn;
> Have sight of Proteus rising from the Sea,
> Or hear old Triton blow his wreathèd horn."

🌾 *Supplementary to page 30.*

Here we have an example of Whitehead's symbolism. Reuel Denney, in his engaging little treatise on "the popular culture of mass media and sports and advertisements," which he calls *The Astonished Muse* (University of Chicago Press, 1957; p. 98), says this about professional baseball:

"Historically, Herbert Schoeffler shows in papers translated by Donald Levine, our American sports pattern is the direct descendant of the Glorious Revolution. It was in the late seventeenth century, especially in the 1690s, that England revolutionized the European sporting ideal. It made the aristocratic sports, especially racing, a social property of all classes; and it permitted the plebeian sports to rise and suffuse the sporting pattern of the whole male culture. The last master fencers in England became its first boxing champions.

"The magnetism of the sporting world in Britain and the United States is associated, moreover, with its meaning as a reaction to industrialism. Industrialism makes men feel a shift or disturbance in the traditional relation to their bodies; they wish to re-create it through sport. Again, as Helmuth Plessner has argued, the relative insignificance of the individual in subdivided industrial roles makes him search for acts of aesthetic completion and expressed, even if channeled, physical aggression. Out of these historical backgrounds rise some, if not all, of the harmonies and contradictions of the American sports world today, especially that part of it which strains to make a commodity of sport in the mass-entertainment market.

"The imagery of competition, as represented in the Big Game and in media interpretation of the Big Game, contributes to the system of expectations holding among various parts of society. Sport can be studied as social imagery—spectacle from which the media draw symbols that are then employed in the supreme court of folkway.

"The integrity of the symbol system derived from sports is largely a function of two things. First, sports recruitment draws on habits built up in the imaginative generosity of childhood and youth, draws, that is, on a pre-class, pre-caste system of social interaction. Second, sports recruitment is a big business with a market to satisfy, a business that trains its own critics and virtually pays to have them trained. These two characteristics of the sports world must surely go far to explain why sports, like entertainment, are usually ahead of churches and schools, for example, in responding sensitively to the moral

pressure for freedom and equality in our society. Thus in the segregation issue, for instance, sports and some kinds of popular entertainment have established community between the races before other
social institutions could or would."

Who Herbert Schoeffler is and what he wrote—in French? in
German?—and who Helmuth Plessner is, Denney does not say; nor
do I have the least notion.

᪶

Back numbers of the *Christian Century* are not easy to come by.
Here is nearly all of Reinhold Niebuhr's article, "Proposal to Billy
Graham" (August 8, 1956) :

"I have no business making any proposals to Billy Graham. We
are not acquainted. But I share a general approval of his modesty and
sincerity in the Christian community and also a certain uneasiness that
his type of evangelism may seem to be irrelevant to the great moral
issues of our day.

"My proposal is prompted by the fact that in the revival which
swept the nation a century ago under the inspiration of the great
Finney, the abolition of slavery was made central to the religious
experience of repentance and conversion. As a result the revival led
to the manumission of slaves in some instances and to various abolition movements in others. Warner, in his book *The Anti-Slavery
Impulse,* gives us a good account of the reality of this type of
evangelism. It sharpened the religious awareness of the central moral
problem facing the nation a hundred years ago.

"A hundred years later we still confront the same moral issue,
though in a different historical context. The slaves have long since
become emancipated. But the Negroes have not been freed from the

contempt which the white majority visits upon the ex-slaves, partly because of their color and partly because of their 'previous condition of servitude.' Men are very slow in their collective life in meeting the elementary norms of the Christian life. They violate the simple commandment 'Thou shalt love thy neighbor as thyself.' So here we are a hundred years after the emancipation of the slave in a new crisis because our government, based upon a conception of law which makes 'equal protection under the law' the cardinal principle of justice, is challenging the mores of the community which incorporated a remnant of the pattern of slavery into its customs.

"The Christian church did not seriously challenge these customs. The political community proved itself more rigorous than the Christian community in guarding the dignity of man. The church, as our Negro friends constantly remind us, was the most rigorously segregated institution in the nation. That segregation wittingly or unwittingly gave a religious aura to racial prejudice. Even now, while many a heroic Southern minister has defied the congregation and the community in upholding the standards of both the gospel and the law, the church as an institution has lagged behind the trade-union movement in supporting the Supreme Court decision.

"It would be idle to mention all this were Billy Graham totally unconscious of the moral crisis in our nation on the age-old race issue. Though a Southerner, he is 'enlightened' on the race issue. He does not condone racial prejudice. But neither does he incorporate the demand of love transcending racial boundaries into his evangelistic appeal. He does not suggest that the soul, confronted with the judgment and the forgiveness of Christ, should regard racial prejudice as an element in the 'life of sin' from which the conversion experience redeems. And he does not suggest that among the 'fruits meet for repentance' there must be a whole-souled effort to give the Negro neighbor his full due as a man and brother. . . . There the moral dimension of the issue is fairly simple. It is whether the Christian recognizes the validity of the biblical observation 'If a man sayeth that he loves God and hateth his brother, he is a liar.' If the issue is as simple as that the question arises why an obviously honest man, such as Graham, cannot embody the disavowal of race prejudice into his call to repentance. Perhaps the answer to that question takes one into the very heart of the weaknesses of 'evangelical' Christianity, particularly of evangelical Christianity in its pietistic versions. This form of the Christian faith relies on an oversimplification of the issues in order to create the 'crisis' which prompts conversion and the acceptance of the Christian faith. The best way of inducing this crisis is to call attention to some moral dereliction of the person, in which some accepted moral norm has been transgressed and the conscience is consequently uneasy.

"The moral transgressions which are imbedded in the customs of the community, the sins which we do not 'one by one' but with the approval of our community, are not such effective means of creating the sense of crisis upon which the revivalist depends. If the 'sinner' is to be convicted of involvement in some collective sin, it is necessary to appeal not only to the emotions but to the mind; that is, it is necessary rationally to analyze the social situation, conformity to which means the violation of the love commandment. This is true even in such an uncomplicated problem as the issue of desegregation.

"Perhaps this is the reason why revivalistic Christianity has not been particularly effective in challenging collective evil. It grew to power on the frontier, where its moral appeals were limited to the condemnation of drunkenness, adultery and sabbath violations. It may not be entirely unfair to observe that the section of the country in which the present crisis in race relations is most acute is precisely that section which has experienced annual 'revivals,' all calculated to 'redeem' the sinner and guarantee the perfection of a truly 'committed' soul.

"I well remember a rather pathetic experience more than a quarter century ago in Harlan County, Kentucky, at the time when industrial violence engulfed the county because of a strike by its miners. Their wages were very low because that was the only way the Kentucky mine owners were able to meet the competition of the Pennsylvania coal fields. The middle-class community was solidly arrayed behind the mine owners. We, who were members of a church delegation, met with the ministers of the county in order to convince them that it was dubious for the middle-class community to be so indifferent to the plight of the miners, simply because they felt that the community itself was endangered by a higher wage scale.

"These calculations in justice, which touched the collective interests and challenged the moral complacency of the middle-class churches, were quite beyond the moral comprehension of the Harlan County ministers. We were assured that they had just had a collective revival in the town and would have another one; and that these revivals were bound to generate the kind of Christian perfection which would make the collective sins we spoke of quite impossible. The ministers were naïvely good men who did not think in terms which were even remotely relevant to the moral issues their community faced.

"The only difference between the situation a quarter century ago and now is that Protestantism as a whole was then informed by the social gospel and regarded the viewpoint of the Harlan County ministers as a quaint vestige of an outmoded form of piety. But now, whether because of the many personal excellences of Billy Graham or because of a widespread naïve enthusiasm for any kind of religious revival, we have official church federations committing themselves to this kind of revivalistic Christianity, assuring us that if only Billy can bring the people into the Christian fold, the ordinary pastors can then proceed to instruct the new recruits in the full implications of the Christian life.

"There is more hope that Graham himself will see the weaknesses

of a traditional evangelical perfectionism in an atomic age than that
his clerical and lay sponsors, with their enthusiasm for any kind of
revival, will see it. For Graham is a world traveler and a very perceptive observer of the world scene with its many collective problems.
His instincts are genuine and his sense of justice well developed. He
could embody the cause of justice—particularly where it is so closely
and obviously related to the love commandment as on the race issue—
into his revival message. The only thing that could prevent such a
development is that it is contrary to the well established 'technique'
of revivalism. That technique requires the oversimplification of moral
issues and their individualization for the sake of inducing an emotional
crisis. Collective sins are therefore not within the range of a revival.
It may be that Graham is good enough to break with this traditional
and obvious technique. In that case he would cease to be merely the
last exponent of a frontier religious tradition and become a vital
force in the nation's moral and spiritual life."

&

As to what I have said about the standing of the churches on page
30 in this matter of segregation, let me quote Reinhold Niebuhr again,
now talking with Mike Wallace. Their conversation has been published by the Fund for the Republic, and you can get one copy
for nothing and more for a dime each. Here's what they said about
the churches and racial segregation:

"WALLACE: Let's turn to some criticisms of the Protestant Church.
You've admitted in your writings that the Catholics have been far
more successful than the Protestants in abolishing racial segregation
in their churches. How come?

"NIEBUHR: Well, how come? I tried to analyze this in an article in a rather heretical way. I said that the churches that are most obviously democratic are most obviously given to race prejudice, by which I mean the churches that have absolute congregational control. In the seventeenth and eighteenth centuries there was a kind of Protestantism that said, 'If you could only get rid of the Bishop, then you'd be a true Christian.' Well, you might get rid of the Bishop and get the local Ku Klux Klan leader instead. That has been the fate of certain types of Protestantism. They get under the control of a White Citizens Council, while the Catholic Church with its authoritarian system, in which the Bishop expresses the conscience of the whole Christian community, says there are some things that you can't do. There must be equality of all men before God in a democratic society. I think that the achievements of Catholicism on race are very very impressive.

"WALLACE: I imagine that you deplore, then, the comparative impotence of certain Protestant churches in this respect?

"NIEBUHR: I certainly do. I said in my article that we Protestants ought to confess humbly that the theater and sports have done more for race amity, for race understanding, than the Protestant Church in certain sects and in certain parts of the nation."

❧

Certiorari is lawyers' cant for an appeal to a higher court—here the Supreme Court—which is taken not as of right but only when the higher court in its discretion chooses to accept it. The word *certiorari* is the key word in the Latin writ which the court above addressed to the court below, "We, being desirous for certain reasons that the record be *certified* to us . . ."

The Court culls through about 1,400 or more petitions for writs of certiorari every year, and hears only those that four of the Justices consider worth hearing, which is something like one in five.

❧ Supplementary to page 45.

Free speaking and free thinking are becoming more politically important as our churches (but not the Roman Catholic Church) relax their hold on the theological tenets of their respective creeds, some going as far as the case of Norman Vincent Peale's credo, which consists of the two words *I believe* repeated three times. (Will Herberg's *Protestant-Catholic-Jew*, Doubleday, 1955; p. 294.) As our churches care less about our theology, the state takes more interest in our politics. The terrain of the *Battle for the Mind* has shifted. This is the title of Dr. William Sargant's book (Doubleday, 1957; p. 170):

"In political democracies it is a general rule that anyone can *think* what evil he likes, so long as he does not carry the thought into antisocial action. But the Gospel text of Matthew 5 : 28, which makes mental adultery as reprehensible as physical adultery, has justified some Christian sects in applying the same rule to all the Commandments. The anxiety and guilt thus induced in the faithful can keep them in a continuous state of physiological tension, and makes them dependent on their religious advisers for daily guidance. But whereas the penitent troubled by lecherous thoughts for his neighbor's wife, or murderous thoughts for his neighbor, feels safe enough in the confessional because the priest is bound by the most sacred bonds not to reveal these confidences to another, a Communist reign of terror is a different matter. Many Chinese plagued with deviationist thoughts will think twenty times before confessing them to the local group leader, despite invitations to do so; and will be in constant fear of talking in their sleep or giving themselves away in public by some slip of the tongue. This ensures that they will take excessive care to do the right thing politically, even if they cannot think it. The Household Police are a most constant reminder of their danger.

"Such anxiety is self-perpetuating. Even the most conformist members of a dictator state are found to suffer from recurrent anxiety, or feelings of guilt; since, with the frequent modifications of the party line and such palace revolutions as make it necessary for the people to anathematize former leaders, they will often automatically think wrong thoughts. And the penalty for wrong thinking is not hellfire in the life to come but economic and social disaster in the present one. This tense atmosphere allows dictators to exploit revivalist methods with even greater effect than the church leaders who first refined them."

❧ Supplementary to page 55.

Here is the particularly pertinent paragraph from Berle's book, *The 20th Century Capitalist Revolution:*

"The corporation is, in theory at least, a creature of the state which charters it, and its operations are sanctioned and in measure aided by any state in which it is authorized to do business. Historically there is sound basis for insisting that the corporation has some color of state authority, its creation being in furtherance of state encouragement of commerce and industry. Corporate action therefore may in the not distant future be held to be controlled by the provisions of the Fourteenth Amendment, which forbids any state government (or anyone acting for such a government) from taking life, liberty, or property from any individual without due process. Where the corporation is actually working under state regulation, as in the case of a public utility, or enjoys some specific state privilege, the tie-up between corporate and state authority becomes clear. In any event, technicality aside, the fact is that the large corporation is relied upon as a source of supply and goods and services by the organized community. If it has power to use, and does use its supply or employment functions to effect political policies as well as to produce and distribute electricity or gasoline, motor cars or washing machines, it has, *de facto* at least, invaded the political sphere and has become in fact, if not in theory, a quasi-governing agency. The actual step of applying constitutional limitations to corporations as such—where their power effectively impairs "liberty" or takes "property"—has not yet been taken by the courts though the Supreme Court has come within a biscuit-toss of doing so in a couple of cases, notably *Marsh v. Alabama.* Elsewhere, the writer has made the argument that when the case is squarely presented, the courts will cross the line, when it is made to appear that the corporation in fact has power, and in fact has used that power, without due process, in such manner as in fact to deprive an American of liberty or property or other Constitutional rights."

You may be sure that the issue in the *South-Eastern Underwriters'* case, discussed on page 55 of the text, was not so simple as I have left it. When the Court corrects one of its own mistakes, there are consequences to be considered and set off against the virtues of consistency. The Court was ruthlessly correct. Jackson called it "reckless" and said that he could not reconcile the decision with "my view of the function of this Court in our society."

> i was astonished
> at the simplicity of the
> solution but as i
> thought it over it occurred
> to me that

                    perhaps it sounded more
                    statesmanlike than it
                    really was
                                                archy

Here, then, is enough of Jackson's dissent to show why he called
the majority "reckless," and also why it is sometimes so wrong for
the Court to be legally right:

"The historical development of public regulation of insurance un-
derwriting in this country has created a dilemma which confronts
this Court today. It demonstrates that 'The life of the law has not
been logic: it has been experience.'

"For one hundred fifty years Congress never has undertaken to
regulate the business of insurance. Therefore to give the public any
protection against abuses to which that business is peculiarly susceptible the states have had to regulate it. Since 1851 the several
states, spurred by necessity and with acquiescence of every branch
of the Federal Government, have been building up systems of regulation to discharge this duty toward their inhabitants.

"There never was doubt of the right of a state to regulate the
business of its domestic companies done within the home state. The
foreign corporation was the problem. Such insurance interests resisted
state regulation and brought a series of cases to this Court. The
companies sought to disable the states from regulating them by
arguing that insurance business is interstate commerce, an argument
almost identical with that now made by the Government. The foreign
companies thus sought to vest insurance control exclusively in Congress and to deprive every state of power to exclude them, to regulate
them, or to tax them for the privilege of doing business.

"The practical and ultimate choice that faced this Court was to say
either that insurance was subject to state regulation or that it was
subject to no existing regulation at all. The Court consistently sus-

stained the right of the states to represent the public interest in this enterprise. It did so, wisely or unwisely, by resort to the doctrine that insurance is not commerce and hence is unaffected by the grant of power to Congress to regulate commerce among the several states. Each state thus was left free to exclude foreign insurance companies altogether or to admit them to do business on such conditions as it saw fit to impose. The whole structure of insurance regulation and taxation as it exists today has been built upon this assumption.

"The doctrine that insurance business is not commerce always has been criticized as unrealistic, illogical, and inconsistent with other holdings of the Court. I am unable to make any satisfactory distinction between insurance business as now conducted and other transactions that are held to constitute interstate commerce. Were we considering the question for the first time and writing upon a clean slate, I would have no misgivings about holding that insurance business is commerce and where conducted across state lines is interstate commerce and therefore that congressional power to regulate prevails over that of the states. I have little doubt that if the present trend continues federal regulation eventually will supersede that of the states.

"The question therefore for me settles down to this: What role ought the judiciary to play in reversing the trend of history and setting the nation's feet on a new path of policy. . . .

"The principles of decision that I would apply to this case are neither novel nor complicated and may be shortly put:

"1. As a *matter of fact,* modern insurance business, as usually conducted, is commerce; and where it is conducted across state lines, it is *in fact* interstate commerce.

"2. In contemplation of law, however, insurance has acquired an established doctrinal status not based on present-day facts. For constitutional purposes a fiction has been established, and long acted upon by the Court, the states, and the Congress, that insurance is not commerce.

"3. So long as Congress acquiesces, this Court should adhere to this carefully considered and frequently reiterated rule which sustains the traditional regulation and taxation of insurance companies by the states. . . .

"The majority of the sitting Justices insist that we follow the more drastic course. Abstract logic may support them, but the common sense and wisdom of the situation seem opposed. It may be said that practical consequences are no concern of a court, that it should confine itself to legal theory. Of course, in cases where a constitutional provision or a congressional statute is clear and mandatory, its wisdom is not for us. But the Court now is not following, it is overruling, an unequivocal line of authority reaching over many years. We are not sustaining an act of Congress against attack on its constitutionality, we are making unprecedented use of the Act to strike down the constitutional basis of state regulation. I think we not only are free but are duty bound to consider practical consequences of such a revision of constitutional theory. . . .

"The states began nearly a century ago to regulate insurance, and state regulation, while no doubt of uneven quality, today is a successful going concern. Several of the states, where the greatest volume of business is transacted, have rigorous and enlightened legislation, with enforcement and supervision in the hands of experienced and competent officials. Such state departments, through trial and error, have accumulated that body of institutional experience and wisdom so indispensable to good administration. The Court's decision at very least will require an extensive overhauling of state legislation relating to taxation and supervision. The whole legal basis will have to be reconsidered. What will be irretrievably lost and what may be salvaged no one now can say, and it will take a generation of litigation to determine. Certainly the states lose very important controls and very considerable revenues.

"The recklessness of such a course is emphasized when we consider that Congress has not one line of legislation deliberately designed to take over federal responsibility for this important and complicated enterprise. There is no federal department or personnel with national experience in the subject on which Congress can call for counsel in framing regulatory legislation. A poorer time to thrust upon Congress the necessity for framing a plan for nationalization of insurance control would be hard to find. . . .

"The orderly way to nationalize insurance supervision, if it be desirable, is not by court decision but through legislation. Judicial decision operates on the states and the industry retroactively. We cannot anticipate, and more than likely we could not agree, what consequences upon tax liabilities, refunds, liabilities under state law to states or to individuals, and even criminal liabilities will follow this decision. Such practical considerations years ago deterred the Court from changing its doctrine as to insurance. Congress, on the other hand, if it thinks the time has come to take insurance regulation into the federal system, may formulate and announce the whole scope and effect of its action in advance, fix a future effective date, and avoid all the confusion, surprise, and injustice which will be caused by the action of the Court.

"A judgment as to when the evil of a decisional error exceeds the evil of an innovation must be based on very practical and in part upon policy considerations. When, as in this problem, such practical and political judgments can be made by the political branches of the Government, it is the part of wisdom and self-restraint and good government for courts to leave the initiative to Congress.

"Moreover, this is the method of responsible democratic government. To force the hand of Congress is no more the proper function of the judiciary than to tie the hands of Congress. To use my office, at a time like this, and with so little justification in necessity, to dislocate the functions and revenues of the states and to catapult Congress into immediate and undivided responsibility for supervision

of the nation's insurance businesses is more than I can reconcile with
my view of the function of this Court in our society."

&* *Supplementary to page 56.*

Where does the law leave off and clemency begin? Remember
Willie's case. Was that a matter for executive clemency or for the
Bill of Rights? No account of the *Green* case—Gilbert Green and
Henry Winston, convicted Communist conspirators—can be complete
without an advertisement that appeared in *The New York Times*
(I saw it there on January 5, 1959) :

FOR CLEMENCY!

IF YOU AGREE

WITH THESE DISTINGUISHED AMERICANS,

WRITE TO THE PRESIDENT:

*(The following is a complete text of a letter sent to President
Eisenhower by the undersigned, among others, and released to the
Press on Sept. 23, 1958)*

Dear Mr. President:
This letter is a respectful plea to you to exercise executive clemency
in behalf of Messrs. Gilbert Green and Henry Winston. Of the many
Communists indicted and convicted under the Smith Act, they only
are still in jail. They were members of the first group convicted in

Judge Harold Medina's court. However, they jumped bail pending appeal and did not surrender, voluntarily, until 1956. They then received three-year contempt terms added to their original five-year sentence under the Smith Act. Of this they have served more than two years, sufficient punishment, one would think, for jumping bail.

If Messrs. Green and Winston had not earlier been tried and convicted, one can hazard the guess that they would not today even be indicted. The Supreme Court in the Yates case limited in fact, if not in express language, its earlier decision in the Dennis case (governing Green and Winston as well) so that the Act now applies only to advocacy or conspiracy to advocate specific acts of violence against the government of the United States. Of this offense there was no more evidence submitted against Green and Winston than against six of their comrades whose convictions were on August 4, 1958, unanimously reversed by the Court of Appeals. That tribunal ruled that the Supreme Court had held "that it must be clear in some fashion that the teaching and advocacy was directed to some sort of action, not merely devoted to some abstract doctrine."

Would it not be in the spirit of this decision for you to extend clemency to Messrs. Green and Winston? In so doing, we are persuaded, you could illustrate to our own people and the world the strength and sincerity of America's faith in civil liberties.

Sincerely yours,

NORMAN THOMAS, N.Y.C.

DR. REINHOLD NIEBUHR, N.Y.C.

DR. JOHN B. THOMPSON,
  CHICAGO

REV. JOHN PAUL JONES,
  BROOKLYN

BRUNO LASKER,
  POULSBO, WASH.

FRANCIS HEISLER,
  CARMEL, CALIF.

AUBREY L. WILLIAMS,
  MONTGOMERY, ALA.

J. FRANK DOBIE, AUSTIN, TEX.

REV. ARTHUR L. SWIFT, N.Y.C.

HOWARD FAST, TEANECK, N.J.

CHESTER A. GRAHAM,
  MADISON, WIS.
BISHOP (RETIRED) EDWARD L.
  PARSONS, SAN FRANCISCO,
  CALIF.
CLARENCE E. PICKETT,
  PHILADELPHIA, PA.
DR. KERMIT EBY, CHICAGO, ILL.
LUCY P. CARMER,
  PHILADELPHIA, PA.
ALEXANDER MEIKLEJOHN,
  BERKELEY, CALIF.
HON. STANLEY ISAACS, N.Y.C.

REV. CHARLES W. KELLY,
  TUSKEGEE, ALA.
REV. JOHN HAYNES HOLMES,
  N.Y.C.
HON. CULBERT L. OLSON,
  LOS ANGELES, CALIF.
KATRINA MCCORMICK BARNES,
  N.Y.C.
BENJ. H. KIZER,
  SPOKANE, WASH.
MAYNARD C. KRUEGER,
  CHICAGO, ILL.
A. J. MUSTE, N.Y.C.
ALONZO F. MYERS, N.Y.C.

(Publication of this advertisement was made possible by friends of Mrs. Henry Winston—Box 113, Williamsbridge Station, New York 67, N.Y.)

❧ Supplementary to page 58.

There may well be some readers who do not know of the Society of Jobbists, to which I refer in the text on p. 58 as a clue to what Justice Jackson meant when he accused Justice Black, among others, of being a "libertarian, judicial activist." I have written about this society before. Some of you belong to it and could tell us more about it than I can. Holmes was its first president, until his death in 1935. Learned Hand succeeded him and is the president now.

There was a time when Hand used to deny that he was even a member. This was not because it was a secret society. I have known members who were willing to talk fairly freely about it, its aims and some of the qualifications for membership, but not its members. No list of its members has ever been published. Perhaps it is secret, but I am inclined to think that the reason Hand refused to admit he belonged was simply false modesty.

Very little about the society has ever been published. In a letter to Lady Askwith on March 3, 1915, which you will find in Mark Howe's biography, Holmes wrote, "This society recognizes that altruism and egotism are only the ways you feel about your work in the half hour's recess, or on the usual Saturday half-holiday—but that when you are on your job, if you do it well, you are neither altruist nor egotist, and that the important thing is how you do your job and not how you think or feel about it afterward. Hence members are to be allowed their idiosyncrasy in recess—if they forget it while they are at their task. It is a club for the abolition of altruism as a requirement of salvation." In another of Holmes's letters, to Wu on March 26, 1925, Holmes wrote that the members "were free to be egotists or altruists on the usual Saturday half-holiday provided they were neither while on the job. Their job is their contribution to the general welfare, and when a man is on that, he will do it better the less he thinks either of himself or his neighbors, and the more he puts all his energy into the problem he has to solve."

This is brief but illuminating. I may add that the Saturday half-holidays were later extended to the whole day, when the society went on a five-day week.

Hand, of course, knows more about the society than anyone except Holmes, and in 1930, on the occasion of the ninetieth anniversary of Holmes's presidency, Hand gave us the fullest account of the society that we possess.

"Are you a member of the Society of Jobbists, or do you know the guild? If not, let me tell you of it. All may join, though few can qualify. Its president is a certain white-haired gentleman with a keen blue eye and a dangerous turn for dialectic. But the other members need not and do not fear him, if they keep the rules, and these are very simple. It is an honest craft, which gives good measure for its wages and undertakes only those jobs which the members can do in proper workmanlike fashion, which of course means no more than that they must like them. Its work is very various and indeed it could scarcely survive in these days, if the better-known unions got wind of it, for quarrels over jurisdiction are odious to it. It demands right quality, better than the market will pass, and perhaps it is not quite as insistent as it should be upon standards of living, measured by radios and motorcars and steam heat. But the working hours are rigorously controlled, because for five days alone will it labor, and the other two are all the members' own. These belong to them to do with what they will, be it respectable or not; they are nobody's business, not even that of the most prying moralists.

"I confess that I have often applied for admission and have been always rejected, though I still live in hope. The membership is not large, at least in America, for it is not regarded with favor, or even with confidence, by those who live in chronic moral exaltation, whom the ills of this world make ever restive, who must be always fretting for some cure; who cannot while away an hour in aimless talk, or find distraction for the eye, or feel agitation in the presence of fair women. Its members have no program of regeneration; they do not agitate; they decline to worship any Sacred Cows, American or Russian, but none the less, you must be careful how you thwart them. They are capable of mischief; for you must not suppose, because they are amiable and gay and pleasure-loving, because they are not always reverent, that they are not aware of the silences, or that they do not suppose themselves to have embarked upon a serious enterprise when they began to breathe. You may go far with them in amity and fellowship; you may talk with them till the cocks crow, and differ as you like and as you can, but do not interfere with the job, and do not ask for quarter if you do—you will not get it. For at bottom they have as much faith as you, and more, for it is open-eyed and does not wince. They have looked in most of the accessible closets, and though many are too dark to explore and they know little about what is in them, still they have found a good many skeletons, taken them apart, and put them together. So far as they have got, they are not afraid of them, and they hope that those they have not seen may not be worse than the few they have.

"The Society goes along quite jauntily; the jobs and the two days off are all a good deal like play. When you meet a member, you are aware of a certain serenity that must come from being at home in this great and awful Universe, where man is so little and fate so relentless. *Fais ce que voudra* will do as well for their legend as it did for the Abbey of Thélème. But they study to find out what they really do want; they remember what Goethe said: 'Let the young man take care what he asks in his youth, for in his age he shall have it.' It sounds easier than it really is to join the Society. I fancy one must learn the rules apperceptively, for it is no use trying to get them by rote; I have tried that way and it does not work. You had best go to the President, for while some of the other members no doubt are as adept as he, after all he has grasped the underlying idea so well that if you get his exposition, you need not go further. He knows about it all, and he is very willing to take in neophytes."

You will note that neither the importance nor even the dignity of the job has anything to do with it. It is not a matter of magnitudes but of attitudes. I don't know who the man was that Frances Cornford wrote these verses about, but I do know he was a member, and I'm sure she did.

> Now when his hour shall strike
> For this old man,
> And he arrives in Heaven late
> He can

> To Peter and the Angel Gabriel,
> Having completely known,
> Completely tell
> What it was like
> To lean upon a gate;
> And knowing one thing well
> He need not fear his fate.

I do not see why he was apprehensive. Perhaps it was because neither Gabriel nor Peter are members, and he was not certain they would understand.

I don't know that there is anything else to be read about the society. What do you think of it? One of the members, Judge Charles E. Wyzanski, writes me, plainly, I think, on a Saturday or during recess:

"I utterly reject the fundamental philosophy of this excellent and accurate portrayal of the Society of Jobbists, its first two presidents, and its recording secretary. The trouble is that you have taken a paradox literally. Of course, when playing a game—especially if you are playing in a representative capacity—you must keep your eye on the ball, and *within the rules* try to win that game. Nothing else counts. And this is because the objects and procedure are defined. The limitations are the condition of the art. Style is performance within the prescription. Or to use a lawyer's phrase, it is 'due process.' Or to take the same thought and broaden it, we can find here the converse of Pascal's proposition: 'Tyranny is the will to have in one way what can only be had in another.' (See *The Pilgrim's Way*, anthology by my second favorite anthologist, A. T. Quiller-Couch, p. 204.)

"But life is not a game. Nor is it (for me) the opposite: a struggle of deadly serious implications. That is, it is not a wager for Heaven or Hell. No such gamble is offered to man. He plays for less substantial stakes—for an ethically satisfactory life while on earth.

"Man has a chance to make a *moral* pattern—not merely something he likes, or something that has the beauty of the dance, or the virility of an ascent of Everest. If he restricts himself to what he likes and the way his taste runs, of course we may get a Learned Hand or a Paul Valéry, but we may get Al Capone or Hitler. And to tell the young to make a pattern without at the same time telling them it is to be a moral pattern is to run the risk of which direction they arbitrarily will select. To advise them to make a *moral* choice is not to tell them *what* choice they must make. It is only to stress that in your way through life you must try to build some coherent structure drawn from the experience of the race, from your background, from your personal insight, a structure that, of course, will last hardly longer than does the theme of a sonata in the mind of the listener."

I don't agree. Morals are not wholly matters of feeling. There is a rational rectitude, even about loving your neighbor as yourself. A member of the Society of Jobbists is not confined to what he likes or to the way his taste runs. He may very well—indeed, I think he will be expected to—admit reason to its part in a moral choice. Capone or Hitler could no more be elected to the society than Martin Luther or Savonarola. Robin Hood would be rejected on both counts.

Supplementary to page 62.

I can cite no authority either for or against the view I take on the power of Congress to enforce the provisions of the Fourteenth Amendment. The Court, so far as I know, has gone no further than to recognize that if Congress were to act under Section Five, a problem would be presented. In the *Wolf* case (*Wolf* v. *Colorado,* 338 U.S. 25; 1949), where the Court held that relevant evidence, though obtained by an unreasonable search forbidden by the Fourth Amendment, could none the less be admitted by a State court, despite the Fourteenth

Amendment, and despite the fact that it would not be admissible in a Federal Court under the *Weeks* doctrine, Frankfurter, at the end of the opinion, said:

"We hold, therefore, that in a prosecution in a State court for a State crime the Fourteenth Amendment does not forbid the admission of evidence obtained by an unreasonable search and seizure. And though we have interpreted the Fourth Amendment to forbid the admission of such evidence, a different question would be presented if Congress under its legislative powers were to pass a statute purporting to negate the *Weeks* doctrine. We would then be faced with the problem of the respect to be accorded the legislative judgment on an issue as to which, in default of that judgment, we have been forced to depend upon our own. Problems of a converse character, also not before us, would be presented should Congress under Section 5 of the Fourteenth Amendment undertake to enforce the rights there guaranteed by attempting to make the *Weeks* doctrine binding upon the States."

Hand, I may add, called it "curious" that "no mention was made" of this section in the segregation cases. "The Court," Hand says, "must have regarded this as only a cumulative corrective, not being disposed to divest itself of that power of review that it has so often exercised and as often disclaimed."

✐ *Supplementary to page 65.*

It was Talleyrand, I think, who remarked that if something went without saying it went all the better for being said. But it does not follow that it had better be defined. H. L. A. Hart, Professor of Jurisprudence at Oxford, came as visiting professor to Harvard in 1957, and he was struck by our aversion in America to precise language.

He said (over the B.B.C. and printed in *The Listener*, January 16, 1958) :

"There is in America I think a wholly different attitude to precision of language, to the nuances that language can convey, and to verbal accuracy. To many Americans we appear to be fussing about the letter and often using the letter to kill the spirit. We stand on the brink, wondering about the meanings of words, while they wish to plunge in and get the drift of whole paragraphs, or some large sense of general purpose, without bothering too much about the precise meaning of what is said.

"This was very much borne in upon me in watching the great classes at the Harvard Law School. The first-year course there on Criminal Law began with an English case, in which two great judges in the nineteenth century decided that a person who was charged with the offense at an election of 'impersonating a person entitled to vote' had not committed this offense, because the person whose name he took was dead at the time of the fraud. Both judges said that they wished they could have held the prisoner guilty of this charge, but that it would be stretching the meaning of the words to do so. This case, I think, typifies all that Americans hate in English 'verbalism' as they sometimes call it or 'literalism.' Blind to social purpose, we seem to follow the empty guidance of words supposed to have some fixed or rigid meaning.

"You might well agree that in the particular case the decision might have gone otherwise without too much violence done to the language. Nonetheless, the type of criticism that you would find of this kind of thing in American books does seem to be revelatory of the relative unimportance in their eyes of attending to the precise meaning or the stable or standard meaning that words have. Often one feels that they think that almost any words will do.

"The effort to define is not one to which they take easily or which they think very important. I remember meeting with some colleagues to discuss the notion of a discretion in the judicial process. This is a matter of importance for Americans, who wonder whether or not their administrative agencies are not too free in the discretionary powers conferred upon them, and my friends detailed a large number of problems for discussion. I began with the suggestion that we might first consider what a discretion was, and how the judgments that we called discretionary differ from other forms of judgments which are the task of an official within the legal system to make. Nothing could have been more repellent than this suggestion that we should assist things by studying what was meant by the key words in the discussion. The thing to do, they said, was to get down to the real problems; perhaps begin with the question—what was the psychology of discretion, how could we ensure by psychological means that the discretion was better exercised?

"If you go to the Supreme Court, which is one of the wonderful experiences for an English lawyer, you will sometimes hear an argument asserting that a case comes within the literal meaning of a legal rule stigmatized by the opponent as a 'mechanical' or 'automatic' argument. This attitude to words made me think that often if you scratch an American you will find a romantic underneath: in this sense, that many have a passionate conviction that if you could throw off the shackles of words and of legal rules and leave honest men to think out what on the whole was the best thing to do at every juncture of life, you would find both great agreement and the best decision."

NOTE: The case Professor Hart referred to was *Whiteley* v. *Chappell*, Queen's Bench, 1868, L.R. 4 Q.B. 147.

᭣᭥ Supplementary to page 87.

Again and again we have come on that affable familiar ghost, called by lawyers "the reasonable man." "That factitious ghost," Hand called him. "Old Truepenny" was the way Hamlet addressed him. It has

become more and more apparent that he, the ordinary man, is the true
prophet and interpreter of our brand of natural law.

I recall to you what Frankfurter said in Willie Francis' case:

"One must be on guard against finding in personal disapproval a
reflection of more or less prevailing condemnation. Strongly drawn as
I am to some of the sentiments expressed by my brother Burton, I
cannot rid myself of the conviction that were I to hold that Louisiana
would transgress the Due Process Clause if the State were allowed,
in the precise circumstances before us, to carry out the death sentence,
I would be enforcing my private view rather than that consensus of
society's opinion which, for purposes of due process, is the standard
enjoined by the Constitution." This is the consensus that Benjamin F.
Wright calls "the consensus rooted in the common life, habits, institutions, and experience of generations."

The common life, the common man, the ordinary man, our neighbor
and our friend, his consensus is our natural law.

This is as it should be, indeed as it must be. From no other source
can a consensus come, except from the ordinary man. But in his
strength as a lawgiver is his weakness. Perhaps this is true of all great
lawgivers. Moses, we are told, "was very meek, above all the men
which were upon the face of the earth." (Numbers, 12:3).

Dr. William Sargant, in his *Battle for the Mind,* makes us wonder:

"It is not surprising that the ordinary person, in general, is much
more easily indoctrinated than the abnormal. Even intensive psychoanalysis may achieve very little in such severe psychiatric disturbances
as schizophrenia and depressive melancholia, and can be almost equally
ineffective in certain settled states of chronic anxiety and obsession.
A person is considered 'ordinary' or 'normal' by the community
simply because he accepts most of its social standards and behavior
patterns; which means, in fact, that he is susceptible to suggestion
and has been persuaded to go with the majority on most ordinary or
extraordinary occasions.

"People who hold minority opinions, even though these may be posthumously proved correct, are often called 'mad,' or at least 'eccentric' during their lifetime. But that they can hold either advanced or demoded views distasteful to the community as a whole shows them to be far less suggestible than their 'normal' contemporaries; and no patients can be so difficult to influence by suggestion as the chronic mentally ill. Ordinary persons also have much greater powers of adaptation to circumstance than most eccentrics or psychotics. During the London blitz ordinary civilians became conditioned to the most bizarre and horrifying situations; they would go calmly about their work, though well aware that neighbors had been buried alive in bombed houses around them. They realized that to worry about the victims when nothing more could be done to extricate them would lead to their own nervous collapse. In fact, those who broke down during the London blitz were for the most part abnormally anxious or abnormally fatigued persons who could no longer adapt themselves to the unusual horrors and stresses.

"This point cannot be too strongly emphasized in its relevance to the phenomenon of political or religious conversion. It is a popular fallacy that the average person is more likely to resist modern brain-washing techniques than the abnormal. If the ordinary human brain had not possessed a special capacity of adaptation to an ever-changing environment—building up ever-changing conditioned reflexes and patterns of responses, and submitting for the time being when further resistance seemed useless—mankind would never have survived to become the dominant mammal. The person with deficient powers of adaptation and excessive rigidity in behavior or thought is always in danger of breaking down, entering a mental hospital, or becoming a chronic neurotic.

"It is also noteworthy that stage hypnotists, to demonstrate their powers of suggestion, make a practice of choosing from among the most ordinary volunteers who offer themselves. The hearty and well-built young soldier or the easygoing athlete is likely to prove an easy subject. Hypnotists are, however, careful to attempt nothing with the suspicious and anxious neurotic.

"The higher incidence of hysterical phenomena among ordinary people under the acute stresses of war, compared with that among the same sort of people under the minor stresses of peacetime, or among chronically anxious and neurotic people either in peace or war, is further evidence (if any were needed) for the point we have been making, namely, that among the readiest victims of brain-washing or religious conversion may be the simple, healthy extrovert." (P. 80.)

&ᵃ Supplementary to page 107.

Term after term, through the last thirty-odd years, there have almost always been enough Justices—it takes four—to grant a petition for certiorari when a trial judge has taken a negligence case away from a jury. This has irked Frankfurter, and when four such petitions were granted together in 1957, he said:

"This unvarnished account of Federal Employers' Liability Act litigation in this Court relating to sufficiency of the evidence for submission of cases to the jury is surely not an exhilarating story. For the Supreme Court of the United States to spend two hours of solemn argument, plus countless other hours reading the briefs and record and writing opinions, to determine whether there was evidence to support an allegation that it could reasonably be foreseen that an ice-cream server on a ship would use a butcher's knife to scoop out ice cream that was too hard to be scooped with a regular scoop, is surely to misconceive the discretion that was entrusted to the wisdom of the Court for the control of its calendar. The Court may or may not be 'doing justice' in the four insignificant cases it decides today; it certainly is doing injustice to the significant and important cases on the calendar and to its own role as the supreme judicial body of the country.

"It is, I believe, wholly accurate to say that the Court will be enabled to discharge adequately the vital, and, I feel, the increasingly vital, responsibility it bears for the general welfare only if it restricts its reviewing power to the adjudication of constitutional issues or other questions of national importance, including therein settlement of conflict among the circuits. Surely it was this conviction, born of experience, that led the Court to ask of Congress that of the great mass of litigation in the State and Federal courts only those cases should be allowed to be brought here that this Court deemed fit for review. Such was the jurisdictional policy accepted by Congress when it yielded to the Court's realization of the conditions necessary for its proper functioning.

"For one thing, as the current United States Reports compared with those of even a generation ago amply prove, the types of cases now calling for decision to a considerable extent require investigation of voluminous literature far beyond the law reports and other legal writings. If it is to yield its proper significance, this vast mass of materials, often confused and conflicting, must be passed through the sieve of reflection. Judicial reflection is a process that requires time and freedom from the pressure of having more work to do than can be well done. It is not a bit of quixotism to believe that, of the 63 cases scheduled for argument during the remaining months of this Term, there are a half dozen that could alone easily absorb the entire thought of the Court for the rest of the Term.

"The judgments of this Court are collective judgments. Such judgments are especially dependent on ample time for private study and reflection in preparation for discussion in Conference. Without adequate study, there cannot be adequate reflection; without adequate reflection, there cannot be adequate discussion; without adequate discussion, there cannot be that full and fruitful interchange of minds that is indispensable to wise decisions and persuasive opinions by the Court. Unless the Court vigorously enforces its own criteria for granting review of cases, it will inevitably face an accumulation of arrears or will dispose of its essential business in too hurried and therefore too shallow a way.

"I would dismiss all four writs of certiorari as improvidently granted." (*Ferguson* v. *Moore-McCormack Lines,* 352 U.S. 521 at 546-8.)

Supplementary to page 108.

Consider the way the Court works. Jackson tells us in his Godkin lectures at Harvard, which he did not live to deliver. The Harvard University Press, in 1955, published what Jackson would have said:

"The routine during the Court term has been to hear arguments the first five days of each two weeks, followed by two weeks of recess for the writing of opinions and the study of the appeals and certiorari petitions, which must be disposed of periodically. The time allowed for each side to argue its case is normally one hour, and, in cases where the question seems not complex, it is half of that. In the early days of the Supreme Court, the volume of work permitted argument to extend over several days, as it still does in the House of Lords. Many cases argued before us today in two hours have taken days, weeks, and even months in the trial court or administrative body.

"What really matters to the lawyer and the law is what happens between the argument and the decision. On each Saturday following argument or preceding a decision Monday, the Court holds its only regularly scheduled conference. It begins at 11 A.M. and rarely ends before 5:30 P.M. With a half hour for lunch, this gives about 360 minutes in which to complete final consideration of forthcoming opinions, the noting of probable jurisdiction of appeals, the disposition of petitions for certiorari, petitions for rehearing and miscellaneous matters, and the decision of argued cases. The largest conference list during the October 1953 term contained 145 items, the shortest 24, the average 70. A little computation will show that the average list would permit, at the average conference, an average of five minutes of deliberation per item, or about 33 seconds of discussion per item by each of the nine Justices, assuming, of course, that each is an average Justice who does the average amount of talking.

"All that saves the Court from being hopelessly bogged down is that many of these items are so frivolous on mere inspection that no one finds them worthy of discussion, and they are disposed of by unanimous consent. Even eliminating these, the time devoted at conference to argued cases is inadequate for detailed deliberation and results, more or less, in a canvass of impressions with the understanding that a vote on any case is tentative and on later consideration may be changed. And not infrequently the detailed study required to write an opinion, or the persuasiveness of an opinion or dissent, will lead to a change of a vote or even to a change of result. If there is further conferring, it is unofficial, usually between two or more Justices of like mind in the particular case.

"The pressure of time may induce an attitude that discussion in conference is futile and thereby contributes to the multiplicity of individual opinions. It is often easier to write out one's own view than for nine men in such short time to explore their doubts and difficulties together, or to reach a reconciliation of viewpoints. The fact is that the Court functions less as one deliberative body than as nine, each Justice working largely in isolation except as he chooses to seek consultation with others. These working methods tend to cultivate a highly individualistic rather than a group viewpoint.

"The individual study which any case receives before or after argument is the affair of each Justice. All receive the printed briefs and record, in some cases short, in others running to a great many volumes. Some records take five feet of shelf space. It is easily demonstrated that no Justice possibly could read more than a fraction of the printed matter filed with the Court each year. Nor is it necessary that he should. But as to his individual labors, with this mountain of papers, each Justice is the keeper of his own conscience.

"In argued cases, conferences are followed by the preparation and circulation of opinions by Justices designated by the Chief Justice when he is with the prevailing view and, if not, by the senior Associate who is. But any Justice is free to write as he will, and there may be one or more opinions concurring in the result but reaching it by different reasons, and there may be a dissenting opinion or opinions. This occasions complaint by laymen and the bar that they are required to piece all these contributions together in order to make out where the Supreme Court really stands as an institution.

"All of this is at odds with the practice of most courts of continental Europe, which make it a rule to announce the decision in one statement only and to issue no dissents or concurrences. Moreover, their work is institutionalized and depersonalized. The court's opinion bears the name of no author. Like our *per curiam* opinion, it may be the work of any member or of several in collaboration. This anonymity diminishes any temptation to exploit differences within the court, but it may also diminish the incentive for hard work on opinions. In any event, I am sure that not only Anglo-American tradition but judicial and professional opinion favors the identification of writers and the full disclosure of important differences within the Court. Mr. Jefferson would have required each Justice to write his reasons in

every case, as proof that he gave it consideration and did not merely
follow a leader." (Pp. 14-17.)

&° *Supplementary to page 115.*

I do not want to leave the Steel Seizure case without indicating
President Truman's attitude toward Congress. As the hearings in the
District Court opened, on April 9, 1952, President Truman sent a
message to Congress. Here is the part about co-operating with Congress, which I take from Alan F. Westin's *The Anatomy of a Constitutional Law Case* (Macmillan, 1958). To read only the opinion
of the Supreme Court is like reading the last chapter first and nothing
else afterward:

"It may be that Congress will deem some other course to be wiser.
It may be that the Congress will feel we should give in to the demands of the steel industry for an exorbitant price increase and take
the consequences as far as resulting inflation is concerned.

"It may be that the Congress will feel the Government should try
to force the steel workers to continue to work for the steel companies
for another long period without a contract, even though the steel
workers have already voluntarily remained at work without a contract
for 100 days in an effort to reach an orderly settlement of their
differences with management.

"It may even be that the Congress will feel that we should permit
a shutdown of the steel industry, although that would immediately
endanger the safety of our fighting forces abroad and weaken the
whole structure of our national security.

"I do not believe the Congress will favor any of these courses of
action, but that is a matter for the Congress to determine.

"It may be, on the other hand, that the Congress will wish to pass legislation establishing specific terms and conditions with reference to the operations of the steel mills by the Government. Sound legislation of this character might be very desirable.

"On the basis of the facts that are known to me at this time, I do not believe that immediate Congressional action is essential; but I would, of course, be glad to co-operate in developing any legislative proposals which the Congress may wish to consider.

"If the Congress does not deem it necessary to act at this time, I shall continue to do all that is within my power to keep the steel industry operating and at the same time make every effort to bring about a settlement of the dispute so the mills can be returned to their private owners as soon as possible."

Postscript

When it all at once occurs to you that you have been taking for granted another prime begetter of what you've been saying, the sooner you acknowledge it the better. Here is a passage from what James Bradley Thayer wrote about judicial review in 1893. It was published in the *Harvard Law Review*, in the school where Thayer taught.

"The ground on which courts lay down this test of a reasonable doubt for juries in criminal cases, is the greatest gravity of affecting a man with crime. The reason that they lay it down for themselves in reviewing the civil verdict of a jury is a different one—namely, because they are revising the work of another department charged with a duty of its own—having themselves no right to undertake *that* duty, no right at all in the matter except to hold the other department within the limit of a reasonable interpretation and exercise of its powers. The court must not, even negatively, undertake to pass upon the facts in jury cases. The reason that the same rule is laid down in regard to revising legislative acts is neither the one of these nor the other alone, but it is both. The courts are revising the work of a co-ordinate department and must not, even negatively, undertake to legislate. And, again, they must not act unless the case is so very clear, because the consequences of setting aside legislation may be so serious.

"If it be said that the case of declaring legislation invalid is different from the others because the ultimate question here is one of the construction of a writing; that this sort of question is always a court's question, and that it cannot well be admitted that there should be two legal constructions of the same instrument; that there is a right way and a wrong way of construing it, and only one right way; and that it is ultimately for the court to say what the right way is—this suggestion appears, at first sight, to have much force. But really it begs the question. Lord Blackburn's opinion in the libel case related to the construction of a writing. The doctrine which we are now considering is this: that in dealing with the legislative action of a co-ordinate department, a court cannot always, and for the purpose of all sorts of questions, say that there is but one right and permissible way of construing the Constitution. When a court is interpreting a writing merely to ascertain or apply its true meaning, then, indeed, there is but one meaning allowable—namely, what the court adjudges to be its true meaning. But when the ultimate question is not that, but whether certain acts of another department, officer, or individual are legal or permissible, then this is not true. In the class of cases which we have been considering, *the ultimate question is not what is the true meaning of the Constitution but whether legislation is sustainable or not.*

"It may be suggested that this is not the way in which the judges in fact put the matter—e.g., that Marshall, in *McCulloch* v. *Maryland,* seeks to establish the court's own opinion of the constitutionality of the legislation establishing the United States Bank. But in recognizing that this is very often true, we must remember that where the court is sustaining an Act, and finds it to be constitutional in its own opinion, it is fit that this should be said, and that such a declaration is all that the case calls for; it disposes of the matter. But it is not always true; there are many cases where the judges sustain an Act because they are in doubt about it; where they are not giving their own opinion that it is constitutional but are merely leaving untouched a determination of the legislature; as in the case where a Massachusetts judge concurred in the opinion of his brethren that a legislative Act was 'competent for the legislature to pass, and was not unconstitutional,' 'upon the single ground that the Act is not so clearly unconstitutional, its invalidity so free from reasonable doubt, as to make it the duty of the judicial department, in view of the vast interests involved in the result, to declare it void.' The constant declaration of the judges that the question for them is not one of the mere and simple preponderance of reasons for or against but of what is very plain and clear, clear beyond a reasonable doubt—this declaration is really a steady announcement that their decisions in support of the constitutionality of legislation do not, of course, import their own opinion of the true construction of the Constitution, and that the strict meaning of their words, when they hold an Act constitutional, is merely this—not unconstitutional beyond a reasonable doubt. It may be added that a sufficient explanation is found here of some of the decisions which have alarmed many people in recent years—as if the courts were turning out but a broken reed. Many more such opinions are to be expected, for, while legislatures are often faithless to their trust, judges sometimes have to confess the limits of their own power.

"It all comes back, I think, to this. The rule under discussion has in it an implied recognition that the judicial duty now in question touches the region of political administration and is qualified by the necessities and proprieties of administration. If our doctrine of constitutional law—which finds itself, as we have seen, in the shape of a narrowly stated substantive principle, with a rule of administration enlarging the otherwise too restricted substantive rule—admits now of a juster and simpler conception, that is a very familiar situation in the development of law. What really took place in adopting our theory of constitutional law was this: we introduced for the first time into the conduct of government through its great departments a judicial sanction, as among these departments—not full and complete, but partial. The judges were allowed, indirectly and in a degree, the power to revise the action of other departments and to pronounce it null. In simple truth, while this is a mere judicial function, it involves, owing to the subject matter with which it deals, taking a part, a secondary part, in the political conduct of government. If that be so, then the judges must apply methods and principles that befit their task. In such a work there can be no permanent or fitting modus vivendi between the different departments unless each is sure of the full co-operation of the others, so long as its own action conforms to any reasonable and fairly permissible view of its constitutional power. The ultimate arbiter of what is rational and permissible is indeed always the courts, so far as litigated cases bring the question before them. This leaves to our courts a great and stately jurisdiction. It will only imperil the whole of it if it is sought to give them more. They must not step into the shoes of the lawmaker, or be unmindful of the hint that is found in the sagacious remark of an English bishop nearly two centuries ago, quoted lately from Mr. Justice Holmes: 'Whoever hath an absolute authority to interpret any written or spoken laws, it is he who is truly the lawgiver, to all intents and purposes, and not the person who first wrote or spoke them.' "

INDEX

ABOUT THE AUTHOR

CHARLES P. CURTIS *is the author of an important study of the Su-preme Court called* Lions Under the Throne *published in 1947, as well as of a study of the law called* It's Your Law. *In addition to prac-ticing law in Boston, he is also an author or co-author of books on hunting in Africa, on the philosophy of Pareto, and on the Oppen-heimer case. He is probably most widely known for one of the most highly praised anthologies of modern times,* The Practical Cogitator, *which he edited with Ferris Greenslet, and for* A Commonplace Book, *a series of wise and thought-provoking commentaries on some of the world's great aphorisms.*

Mr. Curtis has also taught at Harvard, served as a member of the Harvard Corporation, and been a member of that university's Society of Fellows.